D0928105

Club
Drugs

Drugs

Other books in the Compact Research series include:

Drugs

Alcohol
Cocaine and Crack
Hallucinogens
Heroin
Inhalants
Marijuana
Methamphetamine
Nicotine and Tobacco
Performance-Enhancing Drugs

Current Issues

Biomedical Ethics
The Death Penalty
Energy Alternatives
Free Speech
Global Warming and Climate Change
Gun Control
Illegal Immigration
National Security
Nuclear Weapons and Security
Terrorist Attacks
World Energy Crisis

COMPACT *Research*

Club Drugs

by Jill Karson

Drugs

ReferencePoint
Press™

San Diego, CA

For Damon, Drew, and Olivia

For more information, contact
ReferencePoint Press, Inc.
PO Box 27779
San Diego, CA 92198
www.ReferencePointPress.com

Picture credits:
AP/Wide World Photos, 11, 14
Maury Aaseng, 37–40, 54–58, 73–75, 89–91

Series design:
Tamia Dowlatabadi

LIBRARY OF CONGRESS CATALOGING-IN-PUBLICATION DATA

Karson, Jill.
  Club drugs / by Jill Karson.
    p. cm. — (Compact research)
  Includes bibliographical references and index.
  ISBN-13: 978-1-60152-005-0 (hardback)
  ISBN-10: 1-60152-005-0 (hardback)
  1. Ecstasy (Drug)—Juvenile literature. 2. Designer drugs—Juvenile literature. 3. Drug abuse—Juvenile literature. I. Title.
  HV5822.M38K37 2008
  613.8—dc22

                                                           2007018027

Contents

Foreword   6

Club Drugs at a Glance   8

Overview   10

How Harmful Is MDMA?   23
    Primary Source Quotes   31
    Facts and Illustrations   36

How Do Club Drugs Affect Society?   41
    Primary Source Quotes   49
    Facts and Illustrations   53

How Can Date Rape Drugs Be Controlled?   59
    Primary Source Quotes   67
    Facts and Illustrations   72

How Can Club Drug Use Be Prevented?   76
    Primary Source Quotes   83
    Facts and Illustrations   88

Key People and Advocacy Groups   92

Chronology   94

Related Organizations   96

For Further Research   101

Source Notes   104

List of Illustrations   106

Index   107

About the Author   112

Foreword

As modern civilization continues to evolve, its ability to create, store, distribute, and access information expands exponentially. The explosion of information from all media continues to increase at a phenomenal rate. By 2020 some experts predict the worldwide information base will double every 73 days. While access to diverse sources of information and perspectives is paramount to any democratic society, information alone cannot help people gain knowledge and understanding. Information must be organized and presented clearly and succinctly in order to be understood. The challenge in the digital age becomes not the creation of information, but how best to sort, organize, enhance, and present information.

ReferencePoint Press developed the *Compact Research* series with this challenge of the information age in mind. More than any other subject area today, researching current events can yield vast, diverse, and unqualified information that can be intimidating and overwhelming for even the most advanced and motivated researcher. The *Compact Research* series offers a compact, relevant, intelligent, and conveniently organized collection of information covering a variety of current and controversial topics ranging from illegal immigration to marijuana.

The series focuses on three types of information: objective single-author narratives, opinion-based primary source quotations, and facts and statistics. The clearly written objective narratives provide context and reliable background information. Primary source quotes are carefully selected and cited, exposing the reader to differing points of view. And facts and statistics sections aid the reader in evaluating perspectives. Presenting these key types of information creates a richer, more balanced learning experience.

For better understanding and convenience, the series enhances information by organizing it into narrower topics and adding design features that make it easy for a reader to identify desired content. For example, in *Compact Research: Illegal Immigration*, a chapter covering the economic impact of illegal immigration has an objective narrative explaining the various ways the economy is impacted, a balanced section of numerous primary source quotes on the topic, followed by facts and full-color illustrations to encourage evaluation of contrasting perspectives.

The ancient Roman philosopher Lucius Annaeus Seneca wrote, "It is quality rather than quantity that matters." More than just a collection of content, the *Compact Research* series is simply committed to creating, finding, organizing, and presenting the most relevant and appropriate amount of information on a current topic in a user-friendly style that invites, intrigues, and fosters understanding.

Club Drugs
at a Glance

Prevalence

Although MDMA, Rohypnol, ketamine, and GHB have been around for many years, their popularity in the United States dramatically increased in the last decade or so, paralleling the growth of late-night dance parties called raves.

Pharmacological Properties

Although they are often used in the nightclub or rave scene, club drugs differ greatly in terms of their chemical makeup. They are not usually considered as addictive or dangerous as cocaine or heroin, although each can produce adverse health effects.

Laws

To counter the rising popularity of club drugs in the late 1990s, Congress passed several pieces of legislation, including the Hillory J. Farias and Samantha Reid Date Rape Drug Prohibition Act and the Ecstasy Anti-Proliferation Act.

Health Dangers

Following an MDMA high, users typically experience a "burnout" for several days due to depletion of certain neurotransmitters in the brain. Whether this leads to long-term depression and other cognitive defects is hotly debated.

Medical Uses

Both Rohypnol and ketamine have legitimate medical uses. Rohypnol, a sedative, is a legal prescription drug in over 50 countries outside of the United States. Ketamine is an anesthetic that is used primarily in veterinary medicine.

Research

A number of clinical trials are under way to test MDMA as a therapeutic aid in the treatment of post-traumatic stress disorder and other anxiety-related problems.

Crime

Apart from crimes associated with the black market through which club drugs are available, Rohypnol, ketamine, and GHB, which can produce blackouts and amnesia, have been implicated in many cases of drug-facilitated sexual assault.

Overview

> **Although club drugs have attracted significant national attention . . . they comprise a very small portion of the drug abuse problem in the U.S.**

—Jane Carlisle Maxwell, "Patterns of Club Drug Use in the U.S."

> **Not since the sixties has the world witnessed a drug phenomenon like the rapid and widespread emergence of ecstasy and the growing group of drugs that are . . . classified as 'club drugs.'**

—Tony Bylsma, "Truth About Ecstasy."

The term *club drugs* refers to a diverse group of illicit drugs that are generally encountered at nightclubs, all-night dance parties called raves, and other social venues frequented by young people. While club drugs are associated with a particular setting, however, they do not fit neatly into one chemical category; and indeed, whether a drug is labeled a "club drug" is not absolute.

What Are Club Drugs?

In general, experts commonly identify four substances collectively known as club drugs. According to the U.S. Department of Justice's National Drug Intelligence Center and other organizations that study illicit drug use, club drugs include MDMA (methylenedioxymethamphetamine), a drug that is part stimulant and part hallucinogen; the depressants GHB

Ecstasy, seen in this 2001 bust by Swiss officials, is made with MDMA, a drug that is part stimulant and part hallucinogen.

(gamma-hydroxybutyrate) and Rohypnol (flunitrazepam); and ketamine (ketamine hydrochloride), an anesthetic often used on animals. Each of these drugs is synthetic, meaning that it is man-made as opposed to plant-based.

Although chemically different, each substance, according to users, produces effects that purportedly enhance social interaction—a sense of euphoria, heightened energy, or feelings of connectedness between people, for example. Other drugs, including methamphetamine and LSD, are sometimes included in the club drug category since they, too, are often used in party settings. MDMA, or Ecstasy as it is commonly called, GHB, Rohypnol, and ketamine, however, are more closely associated with the rave or club circuit because their popularity closely parallels the growth of the rave culture.

The Rave Culture

Club drugs take their name from the clubs in Europe where the all-night dance parties called raves originated in the mid-1980s. Originally, these gatherings were held in underground clubs that featured pulsing, electronic music. As the movement burgeoned, the parties were moved to expansive warehouses or even to large, unconfined open-air areas. Although quite large, these gatherings maintained an aura of secrecy that many young people found uniquely appealing. By the early 1990s the rave concept had swept to the United States—and indeed, circled the globe.

By the mid-1990s many raves had become mainstream—that is, commercial, heavily promoted events that sometimes attracted thousands of young people. Today, raves typically feature loud, electronically produced music with a fast, throbbing beat. Laser light shows and other visual elements enhance the musical experience—and the hallucinogenic effects of certain rave drugs.

Rave fashion is distinct, too: Most participants wear little or baggy clothing to stay cool in the crowded environment. Many adorn themselves with costume jewelry or neon glow sticks, and some even wear surgical face masks coated with Vicks VapoRub, purportedly to enhance the effects of MDMA. It is also not unusual to see ravegoers sucking on baby pacifiers or lollipops to minimize the effects of involuntary teeth grinding associated with MDMA.

> For many, club drugs are an integral part of [the rave] experience.

Perhaps most important to those who participate in raves is the characteristic atmosphere of peace, love, unity, and respect, or PLUR, as the credo is often called. As one participant put it: "[Young people] go to experience the vibe—the feeling of goodwill and acceptance the all-night gatherings generate. It's a state of peace and unity kids say they can't find in the real world."[1]

For many, club drugs are an integral part of this experience. By some estimates, up to 70 percent of rave participants use drugs. MDMA is particularly popular in this venue; the drug's stimulant properties allow users to dance for extended periods, while the mild sensory-altering effects lower inhibitions and impart a sense of extreme well-being. According to a former rave participant, "PLUR undoubtedly stems from the welcoming, loving, unifying atmosphere that is spawned by the drug Ecstasy."[2]

At the same time, concerns about raves—masses of largely unsupervised young people ingesting drugs that may produce a variety of adverse effects—have placed the issue of club drugs squarely in the public spotlight in the last decade or so. As author Cynthia R. Knowles puts it:

> The rave experience is an uncontrolled trial of the effects of club drugs on youth. A smorgasbord of drugs is offered for sale to a vulnerable and uneducated population of youth who take these new drugs in combination with other drugs or alcohol. There is danger in the product, danger in the dosing, and danger in the mixing. The long-term effects of the regular use of these drugs won't be known for at least a decade.[3]

In response to these concerns, myriad organizations have stepped up research to better understand the effects of these drugs—and their impact not only on youth culture but also society.

MDMA: From Medicine to Party Drug

MDMA was first synthesized almost a century ago by the German chemical company Merck. For reasons that are unclear, it was largely forgotten until the 1960s when it made its way into the hands of Alexander "Sasha" Shulgin, a chemist who resynthesized the drug for recreational use and then published personal accounts about the drug's effects.

Popularized by Shulgin, MDMA gained a reputation among a small but vocal group of psychologists who started administering the drug to aid patients—that is, to induce feelings of openness, relaxation, and connection to others—during the emotionally painful process of psychotherapy. One psychiatrist even called MDMA "penicillin for the soul."[4] In a similar vein, psychiatrist Julie Holland, one of the world's foremost experts on MDMA, has observed:

> Painful and repressed memories typically are not accessible until years of therapy have uncovered them. Under the influence of MDMA, these psychic traumas come to the foreground to be processed and analyzed in one intense

U.S. Customs agents guard more than 1,000 pounds of Ecstasy, intercepted at the Los Angeles airport. According to DEA drug seizure data, MDMA is available throughout the United States but is especially prominent in New York, Los Angeles, and Miami, regions where trafficking organizations are particularly large scale and robust—hence, the amount of MDMA is demonstrably higher in these areas.

session. . . . Any psychiatric disorder that can be ameliorated by psychotherapy can be treated more quickly and more profoundly with MDMA-assisted therapy.[5]

Reports such as these that touted MDMA's therapeutic and euphoric qualities catapulted the drug into the media spotlight which, in turn, stimulated widespread recreational use, particularly in large metropolitan areas such as New York, San Francisco, and parts of Texas. Philip Jenkins, author of *Synthetic Panics*, recounts MDMA's rapid transformation from a therapeutic adjunct into a party drug:

Matters changed fundamentally during the early 1980s as the drug acquired a politically damaging reputation for giving pleasure. Entrepreneurial drug-makers in Texas marketed the chemical as a party drug, choosing the brand name Ecstasy, or XTC. It found its way into the upscale party and dance-club scenes of Dallas and Austin. . . . The media reported that the drug was gaining popularity at an alarming rate and portrayed it as the new drug of choice for the young and affluent.[6]

A crackdown by the Drug Enforcement Administration (DEA) resulted in MDMA's classification in 1985 as a heavily restricted Schedule I narcotic, meaning that the drug has no legally recognized medical use and a high potential for abuse. Other Schedule I drugs include heroin, LSD, and marijuana.

Today, a number of proponents believe that MDMA should be removed from Schedule I and made available as a psychotherapy aid on the grounds that the drug's adverse effects could be largely mitigated if administered in a medical setting. In 1993 the Food and Drug Administration (FDA) approved human testing on the effects of MDMA. Currently under way are a number of clinical trials in the United States, Israel, and other countries that will determine if MDMA-assisted therapy can alleviate symptoms of post-traumatic stress disorder and other psychological ailments. Whether MDMA will ever be put to legitimate medical use will remain the subject of debate for years to come.

> " Today, a number of proponents believe that MDMA should be . . . made available as a psychotherapy aid. "

MDMA: A Powerful High

The most popular club drug is MDMA, most often called Ecstasy but also known as X, XTC, Adam, Hug Drug, and Lover's Speed. MDMA is structurally similar to the stimulant amphetamine and the hallucinogen mescaline. Usually taken orally via tablet or capsule, MDMA produces mood-elevating effects—most users report a sense of euphoria and emotional warmth—by manipulating levels of at least three of the neu-rotransmitters that regulate mood: dopamine, norepinepherine, and es-pecially serotonin.

Effects last three to six hours; users typically refer to this high as "rolling." Although MDMA does not induce overt hallucinations, it may distort a user's sense of time and other perceptions. Although users typi-cally report that MDMA imparts a profound sense of well-being, a range of negative side effects has been reported. These symptoms vary greatly according to the physiology of the user and the amount ingested but may include nausea, dizziness, faintness, blurred vision, and involuntary teeth grinding.

How Harmful Is MDMA?

MDMA disrupts the body's ability to regulate its temperature. This may lead to hyperthermia, a dangerous increase in core body temperature that may be exacerbated by the hot, crowded conditions associated with the rave environment. At the same time, precipitous increases in heart rate and blood pressure often occur in conjunction with MDMA use—and sometimes with serious medical consequences. In addition, club drug users are frequently polydrug users. Mixing MDMA and the other club drugs with alcohol, marijuana, or other drugs can significantly inten-sify the negative effects.

> Club drug users are frequently polydrug users. Mixing MDMA and the other club drugs with alcohol, marijua-na, or other drugs can significantly intensify the neg-ative effects.

A growing body of evidence from a variety of studies with humans and animals indicates that MDMA can lead to lasting changes in brain function. Research on non-human primates, for example, suggests that MDMA in moderate to high doses disrupts the brain's system of neu-rotransmitters. In particular, MDMA depletes the neurons that contain serotonin, which regulate mood, sleep, and sensitivity to pain. Several studies on human subjects have reached similar conclusions: Brain scans of MDMA users showed diminished serotonin receptors, which may result in depression and impair memory and other cognitive tasks.

These studies, however, are not without critics who argue that much of the research rests on shaky methodology, which renders the results inconclusive. These critics assert that MDMA is not especially dangerous; rather, MDMA has been targeted by the drug war primarily because it is used recreationally by young people. As Jenkins puts it: "One therapy drug such as Prozac [legally prescribed to treat depression] becomes a vast commercial success, while another, nicknamed Ecstasy, is laden with sanctions just as severe as those surrounding heroin, though there is little evidence that Ecstasy is any more or less harmful than Prozac."[7]

When taken in low doses, GHB produces a state of relaxation and mild euphoria similar to alcohol intoxication.

GHB

GHB is a strong-acting central nervous system depressant. A naturally occurring substance in the human body, GHB was once marketed as a safe and natural food supplement that purportedly aided muscle growth and weight loss. During the 1980s, in fact, GHB was widely available over the counter in health food stores.

When taken in low doses, GHB produces a state of relaxation and mild euphoria similar to alcohol intoxication. As recreational use of GHB bloomed in the 1990s, the medical community became aware of many serious—and potentially deadly—health problems connected to the drug. Specifically, GHB can produce dizziness, nausea, and impaired breathing. At high doses the drug's powerful sedative effects multiply and may result in extreme drowsiness, loss of consciousness, coma, and even death. A fatal dose of GHB is only about five times that of the intoxicating dose, leaving little room for error in dosing. GHB, moreover, appears to be physically addictive; withdrawal symptoms including delirium, tremors, and even death have been reported. The Food and Drug Administration (FDA) declared GHB unsafe in 1990; a decade later the substance was classified a heavily restricted Schedule I drug.

On the street GHB is known as "G," "Liquid X," "Goop," "Georgia Home Boy," and "Grievous Bodily Harm." Although sometimes available in powder form, GHB is more often purchased as a clear liquid that is sold illegally in vials, small plastic bottles, or even by the capful. Prices range from $5 to $25 per vial or capful. GHB has a slightly salty taste but is otherwise colorless and odorless. Because it looks like water, users often sip it from plastic water bottles or mix it with soft drinks or alcohol to mask the salty taste.

> "Rohypnol has never been approved by the FDA for medical use in the United States. To date, however, Rohypnol is a legal prescription drug in more than 50 other countries."

Rohypnol

Rohypnol is the brand name for flunitrazepam, a synthetic drug that belongs to the class of drugs known as benzodiazepines, which are powerful central nervous system depressants. Rohypnol is similar to Valium, a sedative that is commonly prescribed in the United States, although the effects of Rohypnol are far more potent—up to 10 times stronger than Valium. Also unlike Valium, Rohypnol has never been approved by the FDA for medical use in the United States. To date, however, Rohypnol is a legal prescription drug in more than 50 other countries, including Mexico, Colombia, and many countries throughout Europe, where it is prescribed primarily as a treatment for insomnia. In the United States, however, Rohypnol remains illegal, and its importation is banned. In 1984 Rohypnol was made a Schedule IV drug, meaning it has a low potential for abuse and accepted medical uses, albeit outside of the United States.

Street names for Rohypnol include "Roofies," "Roach," "Rope," and "Forget Pill." Rohypnol is usually taken in tablet form or it can be dissolved in liquid. Users typically pay less than five dollars a pill. Rohypnol's low cost, wide availability, and intoxicating effects—Rohypnol induces extreme relaxation that lasts 8 to 12 hours—made it a fairly prominent recreational drug in the 1990s. Even a small dose of Rohypnol, however, may have deleterious side effects, including decreased blood pressure, gastrointestinal problems, mental confusion, and amnesia. Higher doses increase the drug's sedative and amnesiac qualities and can lead to potentially fatal respiratory problems and coma. As with other sedative drugs, abuse of Rohypnol may result in physical and psychological dependence.

Ketamine

Ketamine was approved in 1970 to sedate both animals and humans for surgical operations. Ketamine's side effects—the drug's anesthetic properties make users feel relaxed, euphoric, and dream-like—made it a popular club drug in the 1990s. While ketamine remains a legal drug used primarily by veterinarians, it was placed on Schedule III to designate its legal status as a pharmaceutical and the fact that it is associated with the risk of dependence.

Ketamine is often called "Special K" or simply "K." Even in small doses ketamine produces powerful hallucinations, a distorted sense of time, and a sense of being disconnected from reality. When taken in larger doses the effects are even more extreme; users sometimes refer to this as "entering the K-hole." Ketamine is available as a powder that is usually snorted, although it is sometimes modified for injecting or smoking. It can also be mixed with alcohol or other beverages. Effects can last several hours. Users have reported that under the influence of ketamine, they experienced impaired motor function, delirium, and amnesia. At high doses or when taken with alcohol, ketamine can cause life-threatening respiratory problems, coma, and death.

> " **Ketamine produces powerful hallucinations, a distorted sense of time, and a sense of being disconnected from reality.** "

How Do Club Drugs Affect Society?

According to Monitoring the Future (MTF), an annual study by the University of Michigan in conjunction with the National Institute on Drug Abuse (NIDA) that charts drug use by eighth-, tenth-, and twelfth-grade students, the use of club drugs, particularly MDMA, increased dramatically during the late 1990s. As Asa Hutchinson, former administrator of the DEA, stated in 2002: "Between 1998 and 2001, Ecstasy use among teenagers nearly doubled. It is feared that the number could double again in another 5 years."[8] Despite such bleak projections, most reporting agencies indicate that the popularity of club drugs has plummeted since the peak year 2001. According to MTF data, for example, MDMA use declined from 9.2 percent in 2001 to 3.0 percent by 2005. Other club drugs show similar declines.

Currently, no consensus exists on the exact impact of club drugs on society. As with other illicit drugs, club drug use can have a negative impact on family, education, and health. Many of these problems, moreover, transcend the individual user and affect society at large. Much of the crime associated with club drugs is related to the black market through which these drugs are available. Managing the illicit production and trafficking of club drugs, for example, involves street-level policing, interdiction and seizure, intelligence, prosecution, prisons, and many other measures. In recent years intense efforts by the DEA disrupted the Israeli and Russian criminal groups that controlled the distribution of MDMA during the late 1990s. The enormous profits in the club drug trade, however, have fueled the emergence of Canadian-based Asian groups that may create a resurgence in MDMA trafficking in coming years. Managing the threat will continue to place a burden on federal, state, and local resources.

How Can Date Rape Drugs Be Controlled?

Historically, alcohol and other drugs have been used to weaken victims' resistance to rape and other violent crimes. Although alcohol is the primary drug involved in these types of crimes, several club drugs have been implicated in the commission of sexual assault. Today, "date rape drugs" usually refer to Rohypnol, GHB, and ketamine.

These drugs are powerful sedatives that are easy to disguise because they are colorless, odorless, and largely tasteless: Each can be surreptitiously slipped into the drinks of victims who become so sedated that they are virtually incapable of resisting a sexual attack. Victims who have been assaulted have reported a common scenario: waking up in a strange room or other arcane location, often without clothing and with a used condom nearby, and sometimes with bruises or other injuries to their bodies. These drugs, moreover, can induce partial or full amnesia, leaving victims with little or no memory of the assault against them—and hence very little recourse against their attackers. No statistics that accurately determine the prevalence of drug-facilitated sexual assault have been recorded; nevertheless, reporting from law enforcement and rape crisis centers suggests that the threat is real.

Many believe that education and prevention is the key to eradicating the threat of drug-induced rape. To this end, a number of outreach programs have been implemented on college campuses and at rape centers to disseminate information about date rape drugs in venues where young people gather to drink and socialize. Similarly, Hoffman-LaRoche, the Swiss company that manufactures Rohypnol, is working closely with colleges to promote education about the dangers of drug-induced rape.

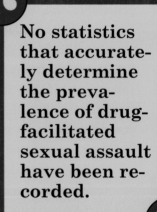

> **No statistics that accurately determine the prevalence of drug-facilitated sexual assault have been recorded.**

Efforts by the federal government may also be making inroads against date rape drugs. In 1996 then-president Bill Clinton set a precedent when he signed the Federal Drug Induced Rape Prevention and Punishment Act, making the drugging of unsuspecting victims a serious offense with harsh penalties. Many social observers contend that this, and legislation that followed, significantly curtailed the use and distribution of these drugs.

How Can Club Drug Use Be Prevented?

Club drugs are used primarily by young people. Prevention and educational programs may be an important factor in decreasing the number of youths who use and abuse these drugs. Today, a number of community programs use a variety of media—television ads, print material, and the Internet—to inform young people about the harmful consequences of club drugs. The Partnership for a Drug-Free America, for example, operates a Web site that includes multimedia activities designed to influence the attitudes and behaviors of young people. The organization also highlights the dangers of club drugs through harrowing testimonials. On its Web site, for example, a young woman recounts how she slipped into a coma—and almost died—after unknowingly ingesting GHB that some-one had slipped into her drink.

Data suggests that these measures are working. According to the U.S. National Drug Control Policy (ONDCP), more than 60 percent of young people polled in 2005 reported that they perceived MDMA as harmful—more than double the number reported in 1997.

Other approaches to reducing club drug use focus on decreasing their availability on the street. According to DEA drug seizure data, MDMA, for example, is available throughout the United States but is especially prominent in New York, Los Angeles, and Miami, regions where traf-ficking organizations are particularly large scale and robust—hence, the amount of MDMA is demonstrably higher in these areas. To counter these trends, the DEA has launched many initiatives not only to dis-mantle trafficking organizations that operate in these and other regions but also to increase public awareness about the dangers of club drugs.

Although club drug use remains at relatively low levels, more studies are needed to assess the abuse potential of these drugs, to foster prevention and intervention efforts, and to develop specific treatment programs that target club drugs.

How Harmful Is MDMA?

❝ The wealth of animal research indicating MDMA's damaging properties suggests that MDMA is not a safe drug for human consumption. ❞

—National Institute on Drug Abuse, "MDMA."

❝ Moderate MDMA use is probably similar in risk level to moderate alcohol use, both with minimal risks and probably overall more benefits than risks. ❞

—Rick Doblin, "Ecstasy Reconsidered."

L ike all psychoactive, or mind-altering, drugs, MDMA affects people differently. In general, however, the sensory-altering effects of MDMA are milder than those produced by hallucinogenic drugs like LSD or mescaline. Indeed, MDMA does not usually produce the extreme behaviors characteristic of other illicit drug use; MDMA users, rather, are generally quite docile. At the same time, the fact that MDMA is not a particularly potent stimulant compared to cocaine or methamphetamine has led many young people to conclude that MDMA is a relatively benign drug.

Acute Effects

Once ingested, MDMA enters the bloodstream and is carried to the brain, where it exerts a powerful effect on several neurotransmitters, the chemical messengers in the brain that influence myriad behaviors and emotions. Specifically, MDMA triggers a rapid release of serotonin, the neurotransmitter that largely influences mood. At the same time, it exerts a significant although less-pronounced release of dopamine, which controls energy levels. Within one hour of ingesting a moderate dose of MDMA, the increased dopamine levels in the brain heighten energy, while the veritable surge in serotonin elevates feelings of empathy, serenity, and acceptance; feelings of hostility and aggression are inhibited. A first-time user described the intense mood change typical of the MDMA experience: "It hit me like a tidal wave. It was incredible: My senses were magnified, the lights became more vivid, the music sounded more beautiful, and my new acquaintances felt like best friends. I didn't even know half of their names and yet I felt I loved them. I loved everything that night."[9]

Adverse Effects

In contrast to MDMA's intensely pleasurable effects, a host of adverse effects have been well documented. Because MDMA disrupts normal brain functions and interferes with many bodily systems, users have reported both short- and long-term side effects, all of which are exacerbated when the drug is used in large doses or for extended periods of time. Short-term physical side effects may include pupil dilation, teeth grinding, muscle spasms, blurred vision, headache, and nausea. In some cases MDMA may cause a significant rise in heart rate and blood pressure, which can be particularly risky for people with undiagnosed circulatory or cardiovascular disorders.

> " The sensory-altering effects of MDMA are milder than those produced by hallucinogenic drugs like LSD or mescaline. "

More pronounced side effects may linger for hours, days, or even weeks after the MDMA high has diminished, and indeed, MDMA users commonly report a "hangover" or "burnout" for one to two days or longer after taking the drug—hence the term "Suicide Tuesday." Experts believe that these aftereffects are due, in part, to the fact that MDMA causes the brain to become depleted of serotonin. As the brain works to build up its serotonin level, users experience a number of psychological side effects, which may include anxiety, memory deficits, insomnia, and depression.

Heat Stroke and Dehydration

Statistics highlight the fact that the dangers posed by MDMA are very real; at the same time, it is clear that they have not reached epidemic levels. According to the Drug Abuse Warning Network, which provides data from emergency departments across the nation, 8,621 emergency room visits involved MDMA in 2004. For comparison, 461,809 involved alcohol, 162,137 involved heroin, and 73,400 involved methamphetamine.

Most of those who seek emergency medical treatment recover; MDMA-related deaths are relatively rare, although fatalities have been reported. In response, the medical community has identified several biochemical properties of MDMA that may result in particularly hazardous—and sometimes lethal—conditions: heat stroke and over-hydration. Experts believe that most of the deaths related to MDMA are related to these two dangerous conditions.

> " **MDMA users commonly report a 'hangover' or 'burnout' for one to two days or longer after taking the drug.** "

Of paramount concern, MDMA can affect the body's ability to regulate its temperature, which can lead to a dramatic rise in body temperature. Called hyperthermia, or heat stroke, this condition is exacerbated by the hot, crowded conditions—and prolonged periods of dancing—characteristic of the rave and club circuit. Because MDMA masks feelings of pain and discomfort, users at risk may be unaware that their bodies are reaching potentially fatal temperatures; remarkably, some users who died after taking the drug had body temperatures of 108 degrees or higher.

Another danger is that MDMA users can become severely dehydrated. In several reported cases, this has led to hyponatremia, or "water intoxication," a condition where users drink so much water that they dangerously dilute the concentration of sodium in their blood. In several reported cases excessive water consumption caused brain swelling and death.

An incident in Denver, Colorado, at the turn of the twenty-first century garnered widespread attention to the very real danger of hyponatremia: High school student Britney Chambers took MDMA as she was celebrating her birthday with friends. To combat the dehydrating effects of the drug, the teen consumed 24 pints of water within an hour. Soon after, she fell into a coma. Chambers died several days later, shortly after turning 16 years old.

> **MDMA can affect the body's ability to regulate its temperature, which can lead to a dramatic rise in body temperature.**

Polydrug Use and Adulteration

Part of the reason that no clear consensus exists regarding the exact risk that MDMA poses to health is that tablets sold as Ecstasy can vary greatly: The production of MDMA is similar to that of other illicit drugs that are illegally manufactured—and unregulated. Thus, the exact chemical composition of MDMA tablets is virtually unknown to the user. The DEA and others organizations that have tested MDMA report that the tablets are often adulterated with a wide array of unlikely substances, including caffeine, cough syrup, industrial cleaners, and even dog worming medication.

Many of these adulterants multiply the negative effects of MDMA or produce effects that have no relation to MDMA, making it difficult to assess the aftereffects of the drug. Perhaps even more important, the amount of MDMA in any given tablet varies greatly. The DEA has found that some tablets do not even contain MDMA but rather drugs such as amphetamine and even LSD. Other tablets contain a mix of MDMA and other potent drugs. As one Miami police officer who worked the rave scene put it: "The bottom line is, kids don't know what they're taking."[10]

In addition to the possibility that MDMA users may unknowingly ingest other drugs that are sold as MDMA, many MDMA users are polydrug users; that is, they intentionally combine MDMA with alcohol, marijuana, or other club drugs like ketamine or GHB. The effects of these various drugs, not to mention factors such as dose, frequency of use, and genetic and environmental factors, make it extremely difficult for health care practitioners and others to accurately assess the exact health risks posed by MDMA.

Addiction Potential

MDMA does not appear to be as physically addictive as drugs such as methamphetamine or heroin, and many users report that chronic use of MDMA is impractical: When MDMA is used repeatedly over extended periods of time, or at high doses, serotonin levels in the brain become extremely low, which diminishes the drug's pleasurable effects. As one former MDMA user put it: "The utter bliss of my first Ecstasy experience was a distant memory. Of course, I could never recapture that first high, no matter how much Ecstasy I took."[11] At the same time, larger doses typically result in more pronounced negative aftereffects, most notably fatigue, insomnia, and depression. For many recreational drug users, then, overusing MDMA is unrewarding.

Although few users have reported the intense physical cravings associated with other drug addictions, MDMA can be psychologically addicting. According to a 2006 research report from NIDA, 34 percent of MDMA users met the diagnostic criteria for drug abuse, while 43 percent of users met the criteria for dependence; that is, they continued to use the drug despite knowledge of possible adverse consequences. Almost 60 percent of those surveyed, moreover, suffered withdrawal symptoms, the most common of which is depression related to the low serotonin levels in the brain.

> MDMA does not appear to be as physically addictive as drugs such as methamphetamine or heroin.

MDMA and Brain Damage

There appears to be solid experimental evidence that MDMA affects the brain's serotonin system. What is uncertain is whether the deficits in serotonin receptors are permanent and irreversible, and if so, how these serotonin reductions affect mental health.

Serotonin is closely associated with mood and many behaviors, including sleep, appetite, memory, and learning. A 1998 Johns Hopkins University study that was sponsored by NIDA found that MDMA users experienced irreversible memory loss. In this widely cited study, led by neurologist George Ricaurte, researchers administered MDMA to red squirrel monkeys for 4 consecutive days. The MDMA caused damage to the monkeys' serotonin neurons that was visible 6 to 7 years later in brain autopsies. Likewise, brain scans of human subjects have also shown that heavy users of MDMA had diminished serotonin receptors. Researchers conjecture that this neuronal damage may account for the memory deficits, depression, and other psychological problems observed in chronic users of MDMA.

These government-sponsored studies, however, are not without critics. The Multidisciplinary Association for Psychedelic Studies (MAPS) is an organization that has been at the fore of research into the possible medical benefits of MDMA. According to MAPS founder Rick Doblin and others, several of the widely cited research reports from Johns Hopkins University, NIDA, and other organizations contain serious methodological flaws, rendering the results invalid.

At the center of this controversy is a 2002 study led by Ricaurte that suggested that even moderate doses of MDMA could cause lasting brain damage and even Parkinson's disease, a disorder that causes people to lose control of their muscles. This study was widely cited by the National Institute on Drug Abuse and used in the institute's campaign to quell MDMA and other club drugs. In 2003, however, Ricaurte retracted the study when it was discovered that the animal subjects had received methamphetamine, as opposed to MDMA, due to a labeling error in the lab. Nevertheless, according to Doblin and other MDMA advocates, hyperbolic claims about the dangers of MDMA continue to be disseminated by proponents of the war on drugs, which has had a crushing impact on research into the possible benefits of MDMA.

> **MDMA has been used by a limited number of psychotherapists to facilitate emotional healing in their patients.**

Research that addresses these and other issues is under way. A massive research project in the Netherlands, for example, is tracking MDMA users over time in an effort to gain a clearer picture of MDMA's effect on the central nervous system.

MDMA as a Therapeutic Aid

MDMA has been used by a limited number of psychotherapists to facilitate emotional healing in their patients. The use of MDMA in psychotherapy ceased, at least overtly, in 1985 when MDMA became illegal—classified as a Schedule I drug with no accepted medical use and high potential for abuse—after a number of scientists charged that it caused irreversible brain damage. Today, however, a small but growing number of doctors and psychologists remain committed to convincing the government that MDMA's illegal status is unjustified on the grounds that the drug can be used to treat an array of debilitating psychological disorders.

> " **Scientists, doctors, and social critics overwhelmingly agree that MDMA can cause dangerous reactions when used recreationally.** "

Specifically, proponents suggest that MDMA may help patients who suffer from post-traumatic stress disorder and other anxiety disorders because the drug makes patients comfortable enough to explore painful experiences. As Lester Grinspoon, a professor of psychiatry at Harvard Medical School put it: "[MDMA] melts away the layers of defensiveness and anxiety that impedes treatment. In one session, people can get past hang-ups that take six months of therapy to untangle."[12]

A New Direction in MDMA Research

Despite the array of opinions that surround this complex drug, scientists, doctors, and social critics overwhelmingly agree that MDMA can cause dangerous reactions when used recreationally. To date, however, the scientific community remains divided over the exact nature of the dangers of MDMA and whether or not MDMA will ever play a legitimate role in psychotherapy or other medical treatments.

Answers to these and other questions may be forthcoming. In 2001 the FDA approved the use of MDMA in human research trials. The

DEA followed suit in 2004, granting permission for researchers to legally administer the Schedule I drug to humans. Currently under way is the first U.S.-approved study of MDMA on patients suffering from post-traumatic stress disorder, led by Charleston psychiatrist Michael Mithoefer in conjunction with MAPS. A similar study led by John Halpern of Harvard University will look at MDMA-assisted psychotherapy to treat late-stage cancer patients suffering pain and end-of-life anxiety. Similar research in Israel and Switzerland may provide more hard data in coming years.

Primary Source Quotes*

How Harmful Is MDMA?

66 **A number of studies show that long-term, heavy MDMA users suffer cognitive deficits, including problems with memory.** 99

—Nora Volkow, "MDMA (Ecstasy) Abuse," *National Institute on Drug Abuse Research Report*, March 2006.

Volkow is the director of the National Institute on Drug Abuse and a leader in drug addiction research.

66 **Evidence for any functional consequences in animals or humans resulting from even massive consumption of MDMA is weak.** 99

—Rick Doblin, "A Clinical Plan for MDMA (Ecstasy) in the Treatment of Post-Traumatic Stress Disorder (PSTD): Partnering with the FDA," Multidisciplinary Association for Psychedelic Studies (MAPS), May 1, 2002.

Doblin is the founder and director of MAPS, a research and educational organization that supports psychedelic and medical marijuana research.

Bracketed quotes indicate conflicting positions.

* Editor's Note: While the definition of a primary source can be narrowly or broadly defined, for the purposes of Compact Research, a primary source consists of: 1) results of original research presented by an organization or researcher; 2) eyewitness accounts of events, personal experience, or work experience; 3) first-person editorials offering pundits' opinions; 4) government officials presenting political plans and/or policies; 5) representatives of organizations presenting testimony or policy.

Primary Source Quotes

66 Many media reports have focused on the government's exaggeration of the long-term effects of Ecstasy. Though some preliminary research suggests heavy Ecstasy use is associated with slightly lower performance on some neurocognitive functions, many more studies are needed. 99

—Drug Policy Alliance, "Ecstasy," 2007. www.drugpolicy.org.

The Drug Policy Alliance is an organization that promotes alternatives to the nation's war on drugs.

66 Parental fears have been stoked by reports of sudden fatalities among MDMA users. Given the millions of doses consumed each year, such cases are remarkably rare. 99

—Jacob Sullum, "Sex, Drugs, and Techno Music: Why the Rap Against Ecstasy Has a Familiar Ring to It," *Reason*, January 2002.

Sullum is a senior editor at *Reason* magazine and the author of *Say Yes: In Defense of Drug Use.*

66 Often, young people die immediately after taking ecstasy, sometimes even after the first intake. 99

—Swiss Physicians Against Drugs, "Facts About Ecstasy," 2006.

The Swiss Physicians Against Drugs is a union of Swiss doctors who support scientific medical research on drugs and addiction.

66That Ecstasy can damage serotonin neurons in animals is beyond question. What is debatable is at what dose that damage occurs, whether the damage is permanent, and if the damage occurs in humans.99

—Thomas Bartlett, "Ecstasy Agonistes," *The Chronicle of Higher Education*, February 27, 2004.

Bartlett is a senior reporter for *The Chronicle of Higher Education*.

66[MDMA] allows the patient to connect to the trauma in a deeply emotional way. The substance was not outlawed because of problems in therapy, but because it became a popular street drug.99

—Michael Mithoefer, interviewed in Adi Alia, "Ecstasy: Not What You Thought," *Multidisciplinary Association for Psychedelic Studies (MAPS) Bulletin*, Summer 2005.

Mithoefer, a psychiatrist in South Carolina, is leading a study in which trauma victims are treated with MDMA to test the drug's therapeutic potential.

66The idea that somehow people are more open to looking at the narrative around their trauma because of the sort of subjective effects of [MDMA] . . . is kind of naïve because it's so biologically powerful.99

—David Drew Pinsky, "'Ecstasy' Benefit?" *American Morning*, February 26, 2004.

Pinsky is a physician specializing in addiction medicine and the host of the nationally syndicated radio talk show *Loveline*.

66While bona fide doctors supported by one US government agency get ready to dole out . . . [MDMA] as a
medicine, other agencies are doing their utmost to
warn teenagers off the drug. It's all very confusing.99

—David Concar, "Ecstasy on the Brain," *New Scientist*, April 20, 2002.

Concar is a journalist and editor of *New Scientist* magazine. He has written several articles on the controversy surrounding MDMA research.

66My head throbs with confusion. Voices, footsteps, and
sirens scream in my ears. . . . If I could just split my
skull open and reach inside to turn the switch off, I
could make it stop. This is hell. I suddenly glimpse my-
self from above. I must be dying. *Am I dead?*99

—Lynn Marie Smith, *Rolling Away: My Agony with Ecstasy.* New York: Atria, 2005.

Smith is the author of *Rolling Away: My Agony with Ecstasy*, in which she recounts how her MDMA use spiraled out of control, leaving her sickened, addicted,
and at times even psychotic.

66It wasn't easy giving up my addiction [to MDMA]. . . .
I have recovered, but not fully. Now, a year and a half
later, I still struggle with both short- and long-term
memory loss.99

—Nicole Hansen, "Real Drugs, False Friends," Partnership for a Drug-Free America, January 13, 2005.

Nicole Hansen is a former MDMA user.

❝There is no epidemiological evidence that parkinsonism or any neurological abnormality, with the possible (but as yet unproven) exception of mild memory loss, is a persistent . . . consequence of exposure to Ecstasy.❞

—Stephen Kish, "What Is the Evidence That Ecstasy (MDMA) Can Cause Parkinson's Disease?" *Movement Disorders*, vol. 18, no. 11, 2003.

Kish is a neuropathologist at the Centre for Addiction and Mental Health in Toronto.

❝Overall, I feel more connected to life. I attribute this to my two years of experience with MDMA and the assistance in reconnecting to people, music, love, et cetera.❞

—D., "Personal Account of MDMA Easing Post-traumatic Stress Disorder (PTSD) Symptoms," *Multidisciplinary Association for Psychedelic Studies (MAPS) Bulletin*, Summer 2005.

D. is an unnamed 38-year-old who believes that his recreational use of MDMA relieved post-traumatic stress disorder (PTSD) symptoms that he suffered as a result of a suicide bomber attack in Jerusalem in 2002.

❝My experience has been very safe with it, and everyone around me has been safe. I don't know anyone who's addicted to it or has problems with it.❞

—An unnamed MDMA user, quoted in Gareth Thomas, *The Little Book of Ecstasy*. London: Sanctuary, 2003.

This 29-year-old MDMA user is a professional who runs her own business.

Facts and Illustrations

How Harmful Is MDMA?

- MDMA works by releasing large amounts of **serotonin**, a neurotransmitter that regulates mood, sleep, pain, and other cognitive functions.

- Hallmarks of MDMA intoxication include **euphoria**, decreased anxiety, and a general feeling of emotional warmth.

- In addition to MDMA's mood-elevating properties, short-term effects include nausea, chills, and **muscle cramping**.

- MDMA users at raves sometimes chew on lollipops or **baby pacifiers** to offset the involuntary teeth clenching that is associated with the drug.

- MDMA can affect the body's ability to **regulate temperature**, which may lead to hyperthermia, a sharp increase in body temperature. Hyperthermia can result in cardiovascular system failure and death.

- Research sponsored by the National Institute on Drug Abuse has shown that moderate MDMA users may **experience depression**, anxiety, and memory deficits in the days and weeks following MDMA use.

Facts and Illustrations

Drug-Related Emergency Room Visits

According to data from the Drug Abuse Warning Network, a national surveillance system that monitors drug-related emergency department (ED) visits, MDMA was involved in 8,621 ED visits in 2004. For the same year, there were a total of 1,997,993 drug-related ED visits.

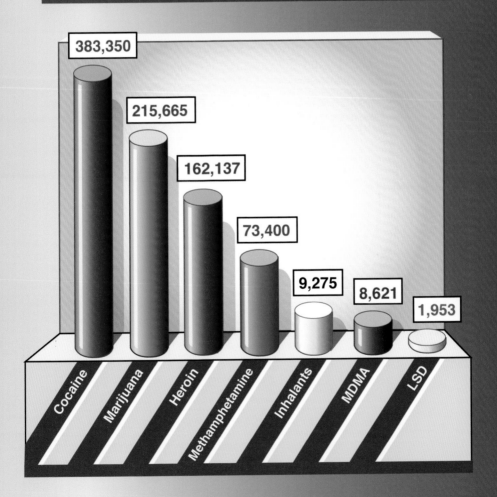

- The rate of **MDMA-related** deaths is far below that of alcohol or drugs such as heroin or cocaine.

- Before it became a popular street drug, MDMA was used as a therapeutic adjunct by psychiatrists, often as a treatment for **post-traumatic stress disorder**.

Cheerleading and Recreational MDMA Use: A Risk Analysis

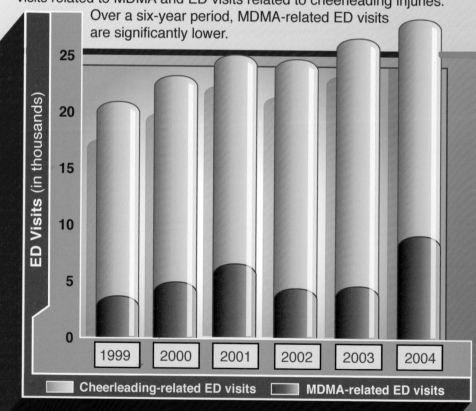

This graph compares the number of emergency department (ED) visits related to MDMA and ED visits related to cheerleading injuries. Over a six-year period, MDMA-related ED visits are significantly lower.

Source: Jag Davies, "Ecstasy and Cheerleading: A Basic Risk Comparison," *MAPS Bulletin*, vol. xvi, no. 3, Winter 2007.

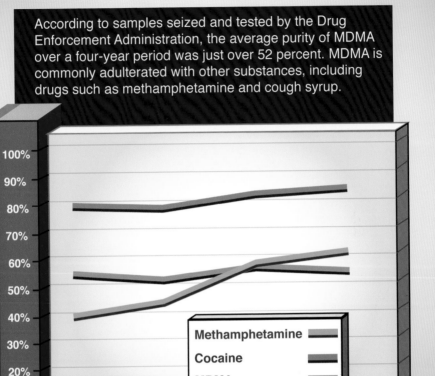

Average Purity of Drug Samples

According to samples seized and tested by the Drug Enforcement Administration, the average purity of MDMA over a four-year period was just over 52 percent. MDMA is commonly adulterated with other substances, including drugs such as methamphetamine and cough syrup.

Drug Purity

Methamphetamine

Cocaine

MDMA

2001　2002　2003　2004

Source: Drug Enforcement Administration, 2004. www.dea.gov.

- In 2001 the Multidisciplinary Association of Psychedelic Studies gained **FDA approval** for human MDMA experiments to study the drug's usefulness as a therapeutic drug.

- **Animal experiments** have shown that high doses of MDMA are neurotoxic and damage the neurons that release serotonin. To date, no unequivocal data exists regarding how MDMA affects the human brain.

Addiction Potential of Illicit Drugs

In this chart, the Drug Enforcement Administration rates the risk of physical and psychological dependency associated with select drugs of abuse. Tolerance indicates that the body adjusts to the drug over time and requires higher doses to achieve the same high. According to the DEA's criteria, MDMA is less physically addictive than drugs such as heroin or GHB.

	Dependence		
	physical	psychological	tolerance
Heroin	high	high	yes
Cocaine	possible	high	yes
Methamphetamine	possible	high	yes
GHB	moderate	moderate	yes
Benzodiazepines (including Rohypnol)	moderate	moderate	yes
MDMA and analogs	none	moderate	yes
Phencyclidine and analogs (including Katamine)	possible	high	yes
Marijuana	unknown	moderate	yes

Source: Drug Enforcement Administration. www.dea.gov.

How Do Club Drugs Affect Society?

"As a whole, those ravers who use rave-related drugs seem to manage their drug use, not letting it seriously disrupt other facets of their lives—work, school and personal relationships."

—Michael S. Scott, "Rave Parties."

"The results of taking part in the drugs widely available in the rave scene can mean addiction, imprisonment, and death."

—Narconon, "Ecstasy: It's All the Rave."

Like other illicit drugs, club drugs can have a devastating impact on many aspects of an individual's personal life; at the same time, they may contribute to a variety of social problems that affect society at large. The exact impact on society is uncertain, however, and experts continue to use many yardsticks as they attempt to substantiate the threat. Foremost are surveys that quantify the extent of club drug use across the nation.

Prevalence

When the rave scene exploded across America during the 1990s, the use of club drugs by adolescents and young adults rose dramatically. According to the Drug Enforcement Administration (DEA), use of MDMA, the most prominent club drug, increased 500 percent between 1993 and 1998.

Data from Monitoring the Future (MTF) indicated that 6.1 percent of twelfth graders had used MDMA in 1996. By 2001 that number had almost doubled. Statistics indicated that Rohypnol, ketamine, and GHB were becoming more prevalent as well. Indeed, the growth of club drugs appeared to pose a major threat during these years; their popularity, however, did not grow as dramatically as experts feared.

> **When the rave scene exploded across America during the 1990s, the use of club drugs by adolescents and young adults rose dramatically.**

In fact, since peaking in 2001 the popularity of MDMA, ketamine, Rohypnol, and GHB appears to be waning. According to the latest MTF study, none of these drugs had a prevalence rate higher than 6.5 percent in 2006. Fewer than 1 percent of eigth- and tenth-graders surveyed, for example, had ever tried Rohypnol. Ketamine and GHB were infrequently used as well. For comparison, 42.3 percent of high school seniors also surveyed in 2006 had used marijuana or hashish at least once, and 12.4 percent of the same age group reported using amphetamines at least once.

The 2005 National Survey on Drug Use and Health (NSDUH), a study sponsored by the Substance Abuse and Mental Health Services Administration (SAMHSA), reached similar conclusions: 11.5 million individuals over the age of 12, or 4.7 percent of that age group, used MDMA at least once in their lifetimes, while the number of past month MDMA users was much lower—502,000 young people, or 0.2 percent of the population in that age group. Data from these and other organizations suggest that the decline in club drug prevalence mirrors an overall decline in illicit drug use among the nation's young people.

Demographics

Young people between the ages of 13 and 30 who attend rave parties and nightclubs are the typical users of club drugs. As in the past, club drugs are still associated—albeit not inextricably—with the white, middle-class suburban teens most likely to frequent these venues. Experts report, however, that this is changing. Data from the Office of National Drug Control Policy (ONDCP) and the National Institute on Drug Abuse (NIDA) indicate that the use of MDMA, ketamine, Rohypnol, and GHB is no longer confined to the club or party circuit. Rather, these drugs are crossing into a variety of socioeconomic and racial groups, including Hispanic and African American populations. Today, club drugs are found on the street and in the home—and myriad social settings frequented by young people, including high schools, college campuses, shopping malls, and concerts.

Although there is no standard profile of a club drug user, several user populations deserve special note. A typical user of GHB, for example, is a bodybuilder or other athlete who believes that the anabolic drug will aid in fat reduction, build muscle, or enhance performance. In one highly publicized case Pete Rose Jr., son of legendary baseball player Pete Rose, was arrested in 2005 for distributing GBL, an analog, or derivative, of GHB, to other players, purportedly for the drug's steroidlike effects. Many users of ketamine are doctors or other medical personnel who have access to the drug, which is legally available in medical clinics and veterinary offices. Ketamine, GHB, and MDMA, moreover, are especially prominent among gay males, particularly in large urban areas.

> **The use of MDMA, ketamine, Rohypnol, and GHB is no longer confined to the club or party circuit.**

Sexual Risk Taking

As with other illicit drugs, in how individuals react to MDMA, ketamine, Rohypnol, and GHB differ greatly. In general, however, people under the influence of these drugs experience a loosening of inhibitions that may result in an array of unsafe behaviors.

MDMA is often called the "love drug" because it engenders feelings of emotional warmth and the desire to touch others. Paradoxically, the drug actually inhibits sexual urges and the ability to perform the sexual act. Nevertheless, many young people have reported risky sexual behavior—that is, sexual behavior that may lead to disease or unwanted pregnancy—while under the influence of MDMA. As one 15-year-old

MDMA user reported: "The way you think on Ecstasy is that you're safe from anything. Nothing's going to happen to me, even if I have sex with this person, and you're not going to be cautious at all."[13]

The other club drugs, too, may elicit feelings of intimacy that, coupled with impaired judgment, may result in sexual risk taking. Users of GHB, in particular, have reported increased sex drive—and sexual activity—while intoxicated. That ketamine, Rohypnol, and MDMA are particularly prominent in the homosexual community is a further area of concern: Gay and bisexual men who use club drugs are associated with high-risk sexual behaviors that may lead to the increased transmission of HIV and AIDS.

Although consensual sex while under the influence of club drugs remains a concern, a particularly pernicious problem has emerged in recent years: Ketamine, GHB, and especially Rohypnol have gained notoriety as "date rape" drugs. Owing to their pharmacological properties, these drugs can be slipped into the drinks of unknowing victims who, extremely sedated by the drugs, are rendered incapable of resisting rape or other forms of assault.

Other Risky Behaviors

Like other illicit drug users, young people who use club drugs may be subject to social, behavioral, and educational problems. Loss of motivation to perform in school or work, failing grades, and unstable relationships are some of the problems that many attribute to the characteristic—and sometimes debilitating—burnout or depression that follows the MDMA high, for example. As one high school student related: "I didn't care about anyone or anything. I just cared about doing my own thing, selling and partying."[14] Another young user recalls how her MDMA addiction sapped her motivation to carry out her goals: "I had come to New York dreaming of a career in the theater. Drugs didn't rob me of that dream, but they did make me willing

> MDMA is often called the 'love drug' because it engenders feelings of emotional warmth and the desire to touch others.

to forget about it. It wasn't that I stopped getting parts because I was using; I just stopped auditioning."[15]

While these behaviors may result in adverse consequences in the lives of young people, MDMA users are not generally associated with violent crime or other extreme behaviors. In fact, some feel that the media has overstated the dangers of MDMA. Users of MDMA, for example, are generally calm and friendly. According to TheDEA. org, a group that opposes current drug laws, "Under the influence [of MDMA], hostility and aggression become all but impossible. . . . Due to the fundamentally pro-social and contented nature of the MDMA high, it isn't associated with the fighting, belligerence, rape, robbery and other violent crimes committed by users of alcohol and (to a lesser extent) stimulants such as cocaine and amphetamine."[16]

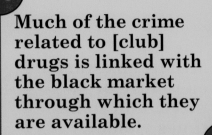

Much of the crime related to [club] drugs is linked with the black market through which they are available.

The Black Market

Like other drugs that are used recreationally, club drugs are primarily available through illicit means, and indeed, much of the crime related to these drugs is linked with the black market through which they are available. In 2006 the ONDCP spent $2.5 billion to implement its National Drug Control Strategy to deal with the illegal drug trade. While no exact figures exist for club drug trafficking and control per se, the enormous costs of the drug war, including costs to control club drugs, place a heavy burden—in terms of money and resources—on federal, state, and local law enforcement, the legal system, and corrections services. Moreover, the very diverse nature of club drugs—MDMA, Rohypnol, ketamine, and GHB are each distributed through varying means—presents unique problems for those involved in their control and interdiction.

The Impact of MDMA Trafficking

Most of the MDMA consumed in the United States is produced in clandestine labs throughout Europe, principally in the Netherlands and

Belgium. These two countries, according to the DEA, produce up to 80 percent of the world's supply of MDMA. In recent years Israeli and Russian organized crime syndicates, once the dominant distributors of the domestic MDMA supply, have been largely supplanted by the Canada-based Asian criminal groups that have become increasingly involved in the drug's transportation into the United States. Smuggling routes are varied; the drugs are surreptitiously brought into the country via commercial airlines, freight shipments, and mail services, among other modes of entry. Some of the largest shipments have been seized along the Canadian and Mexican borders.

> "The sale of MDMA has started to lure organized, and sometimes violent, drug gangs."

While manufacture in the United States remains limited, a number of fairly prolific clandestine laboratories have been discovered in recent years. An MDMA lab seized in Wisconsin, for example, had produced close to 100,000 tablets of MDMA.

At the street level the sale of MDMA occurs largely at raves or nightclubs. As the market for MDMA has expanded outside the insular rave community, however, this method of distribution is changing. The sale of MDMA has started to lure organized, and sometimes violent, drug gangs. In cities such as New York and Miami, MDMA is sold alongside drugs such as crack or heroin by dealers who are extremely profit driven. Gareth Thomas, author of *This Is Ecstasy*, comments on the ramifications of this new trend: "The trafficking and distribution of MDMA is increasingly becoming like that of heroin and cocaine, with the worst elements of the criminal underground in fierce competition with one another. The consequence is gang violence and increasingly adulterated MDMA."[17]

Indeed, because MDMA is not physically addictive, some dealers have begun cutting the drug with methamphetamine or other highly addictive substances in an attempt to hook users—and ensure repeat business. According to the DEA, MDMA samples that were seized in 2004 had an average purity of just 53.9 percent.

Trafficking of Rohypnol, Ketamine, and GHB

The illegal distribution of Rohypnol, ketamine, and GHB varies significantly; each present unique problems to law enforcement and others. Because Rohypnol is legally available in more than 50 countries, and because the manufacturing process is so complex as to render domestic production virtually nonexistent, Rohypnol is generally diverted from legal sources in Latin America and Europe. For example, Rohypnol may be purchased in pharmacies in Mexico and has even been sold over the Internet. Large supplies are smuggled over the U.S./Mexican border.

Similarly, the anesthetic ketamine is extremely difficult to produce; like Rohypnol, it is usually diverted from legitimate pharmaceutical outlets. When the recreational use of ketamine rose sharply in the 1990s, for example, law enforcement officials noticed a new and unusual type of crime: Veterinary clinics and suppliers that kept ketamine were being robbed. Strident efforts by law enforcement have somewhat diminished this supply. Today, most of the ketamine used recreationally is supplied by international drug traffickers, principally in Mexico.

Unlike Rohypnol and ketamine, GHB is easily manufactured in private homes and makeshift labs, even using recipes found on the Internet. GHB produced in domestic labs can be hazardous, however. Amateur—and sometimes unscrupulous—chemists have been known to add industrial solvents and other dangerous additives to the mix. Thus, the exact chemical composition of GHB is often unknown to the user; some have suffered extreme reactions to the drug, including severe mouth and throat burns, seizures, coma, and death.

> " Amateur—and sometimes unscrupulous—chemists have been known to add industrial solvents and other dangerous additives to [GHB]. "

Assessing the Current Threat of Club Drugs

The nation's response to these trafficking threats has required the coordinated efforts of law enforcement, DEA officials, and U.S. Customs services. Interdiction efforts appear to be paying off; according to the 2005

National Drug Threat Assessment report, the trafficking and abuse of MDMA pose only a moderate threat to the nation. In fact, just 0.6 percent of law enforcement agencies identified MDMA as their most substantial threat. For comparison, 39.2 percent named methamphetamine as their greatest threat, and 35.3 percent named cocaine.

According to similar data from law enforcement agencies, federal arrests and seizures related to MDMA have been declining since 2001. For example, the U.S. Department of Justice reports 1,974 MDMA-related arrests in 2001; preliminary data for 2006 shows a sharp decline—just 167 arrests for MDMA offenses. For comparison, the same data set shows that there were 3,557 cocaine-related arrests and 1,667 arrests for marijuana. Availability of MDMA appears to be tapering off as well. DEA drug seizure data, too, indicates that ketamine on the streets is decreasing, as is GHB. Over a million GHB samples were seized in 2001, for example. In 2005, for comparison, just under 67,000 samples were seized—a 94 percent decrease.

In short, club drug use—and the problems associated with it—have declined since 2001, and it seems unlikely that the abuse of these drugs will resurge to their peak levels. That these drugs appeal primarily to young people, coupled with the fact that they remain readily available, however, will keep club drugs the subject of intense public scrutiny for years to come.

How Do Club Drugs Affect Society?

66 Ecstasy has become the drug scare du jour. . . . Increasingly draconian penalties for use and distribution are being devised by eager politicians, making MDMA seem like America's new 'reefer madness.' 99

—Marsh Rosenbaum, "Ecstasy: America's New Reefer Madness," *Journal of Psychoactive Drugs*, April–June 2002.

Rosenbaum is the director of the San Francisco office of the Drug Policy Alliance.

66 Ecstasy use has spread to bars, college campuses, and high schools and junior high schools across the country. What began primarily as an urban threat has now become a national crisis. 99

—Narconon of Southern California, "Ecstasy Abuse Rising," 2006.

Narconon is an international network of inpatient drug rehabilitation and education service providers.

Bracketed quotes indicate conflicting positions.

* Editor's Note: While the definition of a primary source can be narrowly or broadly defined, for the purposes of Compact Research, a primary source consists of: 1) results of original research presented by an organization or researcher; 2) eyewitness accounts of events, personal experience, or work experience; 3) first-person editorials offering pundits' opinions; 4) government officials presenting political plans and/or policies; 5) representatives of organizations presenting testimony or policy.

66 Uncertainties about the [club] drug sources, pharma-cological agents, chemicals used to manufacture them, and possible contaminants make it difficult to deter-mine toxicity, consequences, and symptoms. 99

—Nora Volkow, "NIDA Community Drug Alert Bulletin—Club Drugs," NIDA, May 2004.

Volkow is the director of the National Institute on Drug Abuse and an expert on addiction.

66 The only charges with which ecstasy appears to have positive associations are drug offenses. Ecstasy use ap-pears to be . . . negatively associated with other crimes such as assault or burglary. 99

—James C. Hendrickson and Dean R. Gerstein, "Criminal Involvement Among Young Male Ecstasy Users," *Substance Use & Misuse*, vol. 40, 2005.

Hendrickson and Gerstein conduct drug-related research at the National Opinion Research Center at the University of Chicago.

66 I didn't care about my grades and stopped doing my homework. I stopped hanging out with people I cared about. Every area of my like was affected, but I just didn't want to see it. 99

—DrugStory.org, "Commitment to Quit: An Interview with Kati," 2007.

Kati is the pseudonym for a former MDMA user who related her experiences to *Drug Story.org*, a Web site sponsored by the Office of National Drug Control Policy that publishes personal accounts of people who have been affected by drug addiction.

66 **Out of all the dangers of illegal drugs, ecstasy is of special concern because it is aimed at our teens and youth disguising itself to look like candy.** 99

—John P. Gilbride et al., "Game Over: 'Operation Triple Play' Wipes Out Ecstasy Ring," Drug Enforcement Administration, September 28, 2006.

Gilbride is a special agent of the DEA.

66 **Ecstasy users [in New York] are independently associated with greater levels of sexual risk behaviors. In particular, ecstasy users were more likely than their peers to have multiple sexual partners.** 99

—Robert A. Novoa et al., "Ecstasy Use and Its Association with Sexual Behaviors Among Drug Users in New York City," *Journal of Community Health*, October 2005.

Novoa was part of a research team that charted MDMA use in relation to sexual risk taking.

66 **According to experiments, MDMA does not cause sexual arousal but rather intimacy. People like to hug and to touch each other, but there is no sexual intention.** 99

—Jose Carlos Buoso, interview in Adi Alia, "Ecstasy: Not What You Thought," *Multidisciplinary Association for Psychedelic Studies (MAPS) Bulletin*, Summer 2005.

Buoso is a psychologist in Madrid who has used, experimentally, MDMA-assisted therapy with rape victims.

> **MDMA is available in every region of the country, principally in large metropolitan areas.**

—Office of Diversion Control, "Drugs and Chemicals of Concern," June 2006. www.deadiversion.usdoj.gov.

The Office of Diversion Control is an agency of the U.S. Drug Enforcement Administration.

> **The threat posed by the trafficking and abuse of GHB is low; any national increase in the near term is unlikely.**

—National Drug Intelligence Center, *National Drug Threat Assessment*, 2006.

The *National Drug Threat Assessment* is an annual report that assesses the drug threat status in the United States. The report is compiled by the National Drug Intelligence Center, an office of the Department of Justice.

> **GHB has grown into a multi-headed medical nightmare, draining emergency room services, shattering the lives of those who have lost loved ones to it, and terrifying families [and] friends of those addicted to it.**

—Project GHB, "Gamma Hydroxy Butyrate (GHB): Fact Sheet." www.projectghb.org.

Project GHB is a Web site devoted to educating the public on the dangers of GHB.

> **Ecstasy is not heroin: its users do not base their entire lives around the drug. . . . No, they take the drug at weekends, then turn up for work on Monday.**

—Gareth Thomas, *The Little Book of Ecstasy*. London: Sanctuary, 2003.

In *The Little Book of Ecstasy* Thomas chronicles the history, politics, and controversy that surround MDMA.

How Do Club Drugs Affect Society?

- The use of MDMA, Rohypnol, GHB, and ketamine exploded during the 1990s. Since 2001 the use of these drugs **has declined** dramatically, according to 2006 MTF data.

- Once used primarily by white youth at clubs and raves, MDMA and other club drugs have spread to other social settings and affect a broader range of **ethnic groups**, according to NIDA's Community Epidemiology Work Group (CEWG).

- MDMA is popular among **gay males** in large metropolitan areas. Use of MDMA may heighten sexual risk taking and lead to increased transmission of HIV.

- GHB is used by **bodybuilders** as a muscle-building aid, although it is illegal, and its anabolic effects have never been proven.

- MDMA users are not generally associated with violent crime or extreme behaviors. Most **MDMA-related crime** is related to the black market through which the drug is available.

- Unlike the other club drugs, the anesthetic ketamine is approved for human and animal medical use. Much of the **illicit supply of ketamine** is diverted from legal pharmaceutical sources, primarily in Mexico.

- Rohypnol is legally available by prescription **in over 50 countries** outside the United States; it is widely available as a sedative in Europe and Mexico and is often smuggled over the U.S./Mexican border.

How Many Students Have Used MDMA?

According to the most recent Monitoring the Future survey, which charts illicit drug use among the nation's students, the percentage of students who have used MDMA at least once in their lifetimes has declined since 2001. However, from 2005–2006 there was a small resurgence in use among tenth and twelfth graders.

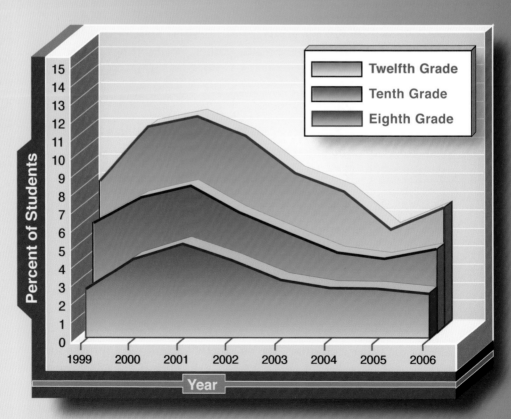

Source: The Monitoring the Future Study, the University of Michigan. www.monitoringthefuture.org.

Illicit Drug Use

This graph shows the number of people aged 12 and older who used an illicit drug for the first time within the 12 months prior to the survey. Use of MDMA was significantly lower than that of marijuana and other drugs.

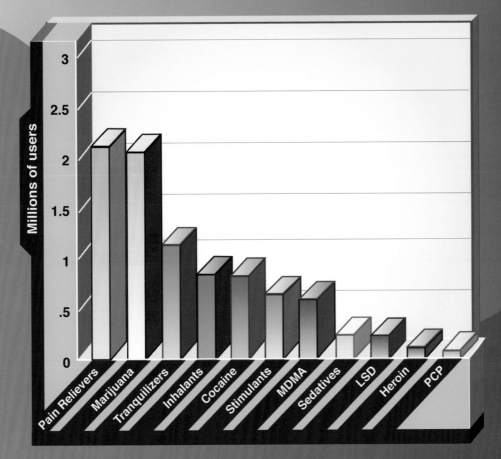

Source: SAMHSA/2005 National Survey on Drug Use and Health

• Most of the MDMA used in the United States is produced in **clandestine labs** in the Netherlands and Belgium and then smuggled into the United States.

How Great a Threat Is MDMA to Authorities?

In 2006, just 0.6 percent of state and local agencies reported MDMA as the most significant drug threat in their region, compared to 39.2 percent for methamphetamine and 35.3 percent for cocaine.

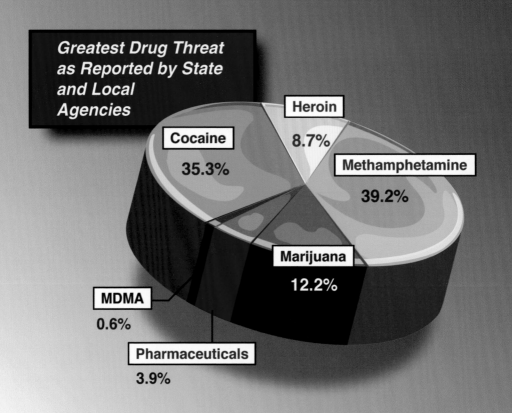

Greatest Drug Threat as Reported by State and Local Agencies

Heroin 8.7%

Cocaine 35.3%

Methamphetamine 39.2%

Marijuana 12.2%

MDMA 0.6%

Pharmaceuticals 3.9%

Source: 2006 National Drug Threat Assessment/National Drug Intelligence Center. www.usdoj.gov/ndic.

- The DEA reported **19 GHB-related arrests** in 2005. For the same year, the DEA reported 764 arrests related to MDMA.

- According to the 2006 National Drug Threat Assessment, the trafficking and abuse of **MDMA and GHB have decreased** since the turn of the twenty-first century.

- Up until 2001, MDMA and other club drugs were peddled primarily within the nightclub and rave community. Today these drugs are also sold by **street-level dealers**.

MDMA-Related Arrests

According to the Drug Enforcement Administration, arrests made for MDMA-related offenses have been declining since 2001. For comparison, arrests related to methamphetamine and heroin during the same period are included.

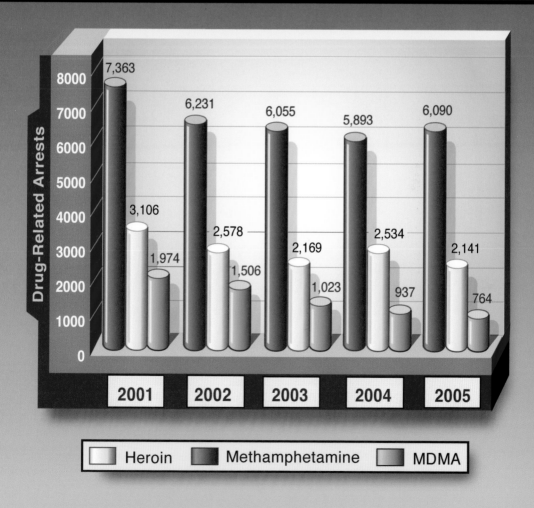

Source: Drug Enforcement Administration.www.dea.gov.

GHB and MDMA Laboratory Seizures

Seizures of domestic clandestine laboratories that produce GHB have decreased since 2001. At the same time, MDMA laboratory seizures have increased slightly, perhaps reflecting DEA efforts to dismantle domestic and foreign MDMA trafficking rings.

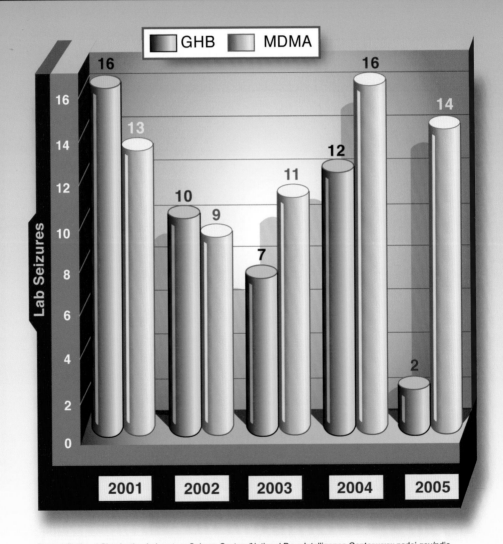

Source: National Clandestine Laboratory Seizure System/National Drug Intelligence Center.www.nsdoj.gov/ndic.

How Can Date Rape Drugs Be Controlled?

> **Nationwide law enforcement reporting indicates that the number of [drug-facilitated] sexual assaults appears to be increasing.**

—National Drug Intelligence Center, "Drug-Facilitated Sexual Assault Fast Facts."

> **Lurid tales of drinks spiked with incapacitating drugs have long been a press favorite, whipping up public hysteria over drugs like GHB and Rohypnol, in spite of such cases paling in numbers compared to alcohol-facilitated rapes.**

—TheDEA.org, "The Curious Case of the Missing 'Date Rape Drug' Victims."

An estimated 100,000 sexual assaults are committed annually in the United States. In many cases the victim voluntarily ingested alcohol or other drugs prior to the assault. In the 1990s, however, rape centers and law enforcement personnel began to report a new pattern of sexual assault: In nightclubs, bars, and other party settings, sexual predators were reportedly slipping powerful sedative-like drugs into victims' drinks to render them incapable of fighting off a sexual attack. As Tracy Duffy and Tina Whelan, who work with sexual assault victims, put it: "No resistance, no screams = all encompassing control. The drugs they use disable, immobilize and silence their victims. One's ability to sense danger is imperative to protect one's personal safety. . . . With the slip of a colorless, odorless, tasteless weapon, victims never get a chance to defend themselves."[18] Investigators tracking this emerging crime have since identified three drugs, now commonly referred to as "date-rape" drugs: Rohypnol, GHB, and to a lesser extent, ketamine.

Ideal Predatory Drugs

The pharmacological properties of Rohypnol, GHB, and ketamine make them ideal predatory drugs. Rohypnol, for example, is an extremely potent sedative-hypnotic drug; even small doses can put users into a deep sleep for up to eight hours and cause anterograde amnesia, in which users cannot remember events that transpired while under the influence—hence Rohypnol's nickname "forget pill." In larger doses the effects of Rohypnol are considerably heightened—and far more hazardous. In addition to deep sleep and profound memory loss, vomiting, hallucinations, breathing difficulties, and coma have been reported.

> The pharmacological properties of Rohypnol, GHB, and ketamine make them ideal predatory drugs.

Like Rohypnol, GHB in recreational doses relaxes and sedates users; many report mild euphoria while under the influence of the drug. A higher dose of GHB can produce an extremely deep sleep—sometimes mistaken for coma—that lasts for up to four hours, followed by pronounced amnesia. At these higher doses, moreover, GHB may cause disorientation, slowed heart rate, seizures, and coma. Overdose is a very real danger, as the lethal dose is only about five times the intoxicating dose. Thus, victims who are drugged with GHB are not only in danger of being assaulted but also may suffer potentially life-threatening aftereffects of the drug.

Ketamine produces a dreamlike, euphoric state. While there appears to be minimal risk of death from overdosing, high doses of ketamine—characteristic of malicious poisonings—may result in cognitive impairment, delirium, amnesia, and respiratory problems.

How Prevalent Is Drug-Facilitated Rape?

Drug-facilitated rape is extremely difficult to measure. As U.S. Department of Justice attorneys Nora Fitzgerald and K. Jack Riley stated in a 2000 report: "No one really knows how common drug-facilitated rape is because today's research tools do not offer a means of measuring the number of incidents."[19] Today the situation remains largely unchanged—that is, there is no single federal data base that captures the incidence of this offense. Although the true scope of the problem remains unknown, data from law enforcement, victims' advocacy groups, the medical community, and the victims themselves provide valuable information that clearly indicates that the risk of drug-facilitated assault is real, if not easily quantified.

Anecdotal evidence from a variety of sources provides some insight into the prevalence of this type of crime. Out of nearly 300 women who called a rape crisis center in Boston in 2005, for example, 68 women believed they were drugged with Rohypnol or GHB prior to their assault—a 30 percent increase from the year before. Similarly, police officers in San Jose report that several times a month they hear allegations from women who believe that someone deliberately put a drug in their drink

> " Drug-facilitated rape is extremely difficult to measure. "

to disable them. In general, however, only anecdotal evidence exists to substantiate these and similar allegations that are frequently reported in the media.

Current and proposed research may provide necessary data. In 2006, for example, a study conducted at the University of Illinois at Chicago and funded by the National Institute of Justice reported that almost 5 percent of rape victims—out of a pool of 144 subjects in Texas, California, Minnesota, and Washington—were given date rape drugs prior to their assault.

Data from the Drug Abuse Warning Network (DAWN), which tracks information related to emergency room visits, provides more useful information on these drugs' prevalence in society. In 2004 nearly 2 million emergency department visits were drug related. Of these, GHB was involved in 2,340 visits, Rohypnol in 473 visits, and ketamine in 227 visits. Data from Monitoring the Future (MTF), the annual study that tracks voluntary use of illicit drugs, appears to corroborate these relatively low numbers: In 2006 no more than 1.1 percent of students surveyed reported using Rohypnol or GHB during the past year, and just 1.4 percent reported using ketamine.

Law Enforcement Challenges

According to the National Bureau of Crime Statistics, only 40 percent of all rapes that occur are reported; only 50 percent of these will lead to an arrest. In terms of drug-facilitated sexual assault, the numbers may be much lower, and indeed, the very nature of date rape drugs presents myriad challenges to law enforcement personnel. Most criminal investigations depend in large part on the victim's ability to supply information about the crime. Drugged victims, however, have no memory—or seriously impaired memory—of the assault against them, rendering this crucial source of information almost nonexistent. As a former New York City police officer put it: "How about a case where the victim tells you she knows a crime has been committed against her but can't tell you who did it, where it happened, when it happened, how it happened, or why it happened? Every investigator will be called to task when looking into a date rape drug."[20]

> **The number of people who believe they have been drugged for sexual purposes is high.**

Another reason that it is so difficult to gauge the incidence of drug-facilitated assault is that conclusive forensic evidence is often lacking. Toxicology tests that detect the presence of date rape drugs in blood and urine, for example, are a vital source of information. These drugs, however, are rapidly metabolized: Each leaves a user's body in under 72 hours. Evidence of GHB in a victim's system may be lost in as little as 8 hours. Because of the amnesiac effects of these drugs, many victims do not seek help until it is too late—that is, when all traces of date rape drugs are no longer detectable. At the same time, many jurisdictions do not even include toxicology tests as part of their forensic rape kits, which typically collect DNA, for example. Many rape centers and other victim advocates are calling for toxicology tests that determine the presence of date rape drugs to become a standard component of rape exams.

In short, the number of people who believe they have been drugged for sexual purposes is high, and hard data to prove these charges remains elusive. Evidence is mounting, moreover, that date rape drugging is not always for the commission of a sexual crime. In 2006, for example, an Illinois man was charged with smothering his wife to death after drugging her with GHB so that she would be unable to fend off the attack. Other victims have reported being robbed after they were sedated with these drugs.

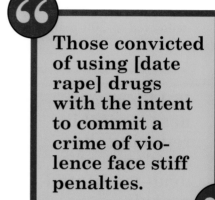

Those convicted of using [date rape] drugs with the intent to commit a crime of violence face stiff penalties.

Prevention Strategies at the Federal Level

As drug-facilitated rape came into sharp focus in the 1990s, federal policy makers took swift action to address the threat. In 1996 then-president Bill Clinton signed the Drug Induced Rape and Punishment Act, which provides harsh criminal penalties—up to 20 years in prison—for anyone convicted of using drugs in the commission of rape or other violent crime.

The highly publicized deaths of two young girls spurred renewed federal action. In 1996, 17-year-old Hillory J. Farias of Texas died after unknowingly drinking a beverage spiked with GHB. Three years later a Michigan teen named Samantha Reid suffered the same fate: Reid was just 15 years old when some boys from her high school slipped GHB into her soda. After losing consciousness she was taken to a hospital, where she died 18 hours later.

In the wake of these deaths Congress passed the Hillory J. Farias and Samantha Reid Date Rape Prohibition Act in February 2000, making GHB a Schedule I drug, the most restrictive classification for a controlled substance. The act also required the secretary of Health and Human Services to develop programs to educate the public about date rape drugs.

Raising the penalties associated with date rape drugs considerably expanded the powers of law enforcement and the legal system. Today those convicted of using these drugs with the intent to commit a crime of violence face stiff penalties. In 2006, for example, a Florida man was sentenced to 200 years—20 years on each of 10 federal counts against him—for using GHB to sedate and then sexually assault a number of gay men in the state.

> **Public awareness is vital in reducing the incidence of drug-facilitated assault.**

Campaigns to Raise Awareness

Public awareness is vital in reducing the incidence of drug-facilitated assault. To this end a number of organizations have launched campaigns to alert high-risk groups—primarily teens and young adults who attend clubs and other social gatherings—to the dangers of date rape drugs. These programs generally address three issues: First, they exhort young people to follow commonsense precautions. To reduce the risk of surreptitious drugging, for example, clubbers and partygoers are warned not to leave drinks unattended, not to accept drinks from strangers, and to subscribe to the buddy system. Second, these programs help potential victims recognize signs that they may have been drugged: Difficulty walking or talking, memory lapses, hallucinations, and hangover despite having ingested little or no alcohol are all hallmarks of date rape drug intoxication. Finally, these programs provide information to victims who suspect that they may have been drugged and/or sexually assaulted, including where to go for help and how to preserve forensic evidence so that the incident can be investigated.

One such program is the "Watch Your Drink–Watch Your Friend" campaign launched by the Doris Tate Crime Victims' Foundation in California in partnership with the Women's Resource Center at California State University in Sacramento. To promote public awareness, stickers and posters printed with information about the effects and dangers of predatory drugs are placed in college dormitories. Similarly, coasters, brochures, and posters are distributed to nightclubs and other places frequented by young people.

Other programs approach the problem from a different perspective—that is, they attempt to dissuade would-be predators from using these drugs. A poster distributed by the Drug Enforcement Administration, for example, shows the woeful image of a man behind prison bars and a caption that reads, "Use a Date Rape Drug and Enjoy One Night of Pleasure. And Regret It for 20 Years."

Other Measures to Combat Drug-Facilitated Rape

To complement public education campaigns and law enforcement strategies that target date rape drugs, a number of private businesses and other organizations have stepped to the fore. In 1997, for example, Hoffman-LaRoche, the manufacturer of Rohypnol, reformulated the drug to release a blue dye when mixed with liquid and take longer to dissolve, making it easier to detect and therefore less likely to be involuntarily ingested. Because Rohypnol does not appear on standard drug tests, moreover, Hoffman-LaRoche has developed an inexpensive test to detect Rohypnol in the body—information that is crucial to law enforcement agencies and legal workers involved in these types of crimes. Other efforts to fetter date rape poisonings involve portable drug tests.

> More accurate tracking of drug-facilitated rape may one day substantiate the threat that these drugs pose.

For example, a company called Drink Safe Technologies recently developed its "Date Rape Drug Spotter," a cardboard drink coaster that is designed to change color to indicate the presence of ketamine or GHB. The Date Rape Drug Spotter enables users to easily and discretely test their beverages by placing a drop of liquid on the coaster. Similarly, in 2004 a British company introduced a pocket-sized test kit that changes color when it comes into contact with a liquid that has been spiked with GHB or ketamine.

Today, stories about drug-facilitated rape continue to make the headlines. Some social critics contend that sensationalized reporting—in which these drugs are presented as nothing short of rape facilitators—overstates the threat, and that in reality these drugs are most often used for recreational purposes. Others vehemently disagree with this position and feel that society must utilize all of its resources to protect the general public from these drugs. More accurate tracking of drug-facilitated rape may one day substantiate the threat that these drugs pose—and lead to more effective campaigns against them.

Primary Source Quotes*

How Can Date Rape Drugs Be Controlled?

66 **Over the course of the past several years, rape crisis centers, college campuses and law enforcement agencies throughout the nation have been plagued with increasing reports of suspected drug 'dosing' and drug induced sexual assaults.** 99

—Watch Your Drink–Watch Your Friends, "Watch Your Drink–Watch Your Friends: An Educational Program Addressing the Issue of Drug Facilitated Sexual Assault," March 12, 2007.

Watch Your Drink–Watch Your Friends is an educational program that disseminates information about predatory drugs.

66 **The tasteless and odorless depressants Rohypnol and GHB are often used in the commission of sexual assaults.** 99

—Drug Enforcement Administration, "Club Drugs," 2006.

The Drug Enforcement Administration, a branch of the Justice Department, is the nation's chief antidrug enforcement agency.

* Editor's Note: While the definition of a primary source can be narrowly or broadly defined, for the purposes of Compact Research, a primary source consists of: 1) results of original research presented by an organization or researcher; 2) eyewitness accounts of events, personal experience, or work experience; 3) first-person editorials offering pundits' opinions; 4) government officials presenting political plans and/or policies; 5) representatives of organizations presenting testimony or policy.

66It's not clear exactly how often rapists use GHB or Ro-hypnol, but such cases are surely much rarer than the hysterical reaction from the press and Congress . . . would lead one to believe.99

—Jacob Sullum, "Sex, Drugs, and Techno Music: Why the Rap Against Ecstasy Has a Familiar Ring to It," *Reason*, January 2002.

Sullum is a senior editor at *Reason* magazine and the author of *Say Yes: In Defense of Drug Use*.

66Determining the prevalence of drink spiking is ex-tremely difficult. Studies are rare and frequently have questionable findings, with some claiming that as many as 1-in-4 women have been sexually assaulted after having their drink spiked.99

—Angie Rankman, "Drink Spiking? It Used to Be Called Rape," May 8, 2006. www.aphroditewomenshealth.com.

Rankman is a contributor to *Aphrodite Women's Health*, a Web-based publication that disseminates information related to health issues that affect women.

66Drink spiking is a crime that the police cannot solve. . . . It is simply too easy to put something into your drink—no matter how vigilant you are. Deterrence, not arrests and convictions, is the key to solving drink-spiking crimes.99

—Drink Detective, "The Drink Detective Program to Reduce Drink Spiking in Public Drinking Establishments," 2005. www.drinkdetective.com.

The Drink Detective is a portable, pocket-sized test to detect the presence of the most commonly abused date rape drugs.

❝Drink-spiking awareness campaigns aren't just wrong-headed. . . . They play on people's anxieties. The message is: he seems nice, but can you really trust him? Look who's behind you.❞

—Josie Appleton, "Drink-Spiking Scare: Shots of Anxiety," *Spiked*, December 8, 2005.

Appleton, a journalist, writes for a variety of publications in the United Kingdom.

❝I was completely naked and had no idea how long I had been there or what had been done to me. Suddenly, I was wrenched up and . . . [raped.] I knew what was happening but couldn't do anything.❞

—Jessica du-Cille, in Samantha Wostear, "He Seemed the Perfect Gent . . . Then He Drugged My Drink and Raped Me,"
Sun Newspaper Online, 2006.

Du-Cille is a 31-year-old secretary who was raped by several men after her drink was surreptitiously drugged at a nightclub.

❝The reality is harsh—'date rape' and drug facilitated assault can happen to anyone, regardless of their gender, age, [or] socio-economic status.❞

—Tracy Duffy and Tina Whelan, "The Truth About 'Date Rape' Drugs," 2006. www.coalitionagainstviolence.ca.

Duffy coordinates a sexual assault crisis and prevention center, and Whalen coordinates a sexual assault nurse examiners program.

66 **Rapists now have in their lurid arsenal more than a couple of methods to render their victims helpless.** 99

—John DePresca, "Date Rape Drugs," *Law & Order*, October 31, 2003.

DePresca is a former New York City police officer.

66 **Although popular media presentations of date related drugs labels Rohypnol and GHB as the common date rape drugs, . . . alcohol is the most common finding in investigations of drug-facilitated sexual assault cases.** 99

—Monterey Rape Crisis Center, "Fact Sheet," 2006.

The Monterey Rape Crisis Center provides support for victims of sexual assault and seeks to prevent sexual violence through education.

66 **Although . . . [Rohypnol] has gained a name in America as the 'date rape' drug, known cases of drugging are relatively rare and the drug is mostly used recreationally.** 99

—Drug Policy Alliance, "Club Drugs," 2007. www.drugpolicy.org.

The Drug Policy Alliance is an organization working to reform the nation's drug policies.

66 As demonstrated in this study [of drug related sexual assault], the subject's own drug usage was more likely a factor in facilitating a sexual assault rather than surreptitious drugging. 99

—Adam Negrusz et al., "Estimate of the Incidence of Drug-Facilitated Sexual Assault in the U.S.," Chicago: University of Illinois at Chicago, June 2, 2005.

Negrusz, sponsored by the U.S. Department of Justice, prepared this report on drug-facilitated sexual assault.

How Can Date Rape Drugs Be Controlled?

- Because they produce memory loss and blackouts, GHB, ketamine, and Rohypnol have been used to **incapacitate** victims for the purpose of sexual assault.

- More than any other club drug, **GHB is easy to overdose on**, since the lethal dose is only slightly higher than the intoxicating dose.

- The sedative effects of GHB, ketamine, and Rohypnol are greatly exacerbated by the concurrent **use of alcohol**.

- A 2006 study by the University of Illinois reported that **5 percent** of the rape victims monitored had been given a date rape drug prior to being assaulted.

- Many drug-facilitated assaults go undetected, primarily because the drugs can produce **profound amnesia**; victims may have no memory that they were assaulted.

- Some date rape drugs are rapidly metabolized: GHB is cleared from the body in **8 hours** or less; ketamine leaves the body in **24 hours** or less; traces of Rohypnol may remain in the system for up to **72 hours**.

- Some date rape druggings involve crimes other than **sexual assault**, such as robbery.

- In 2004 ketamine was involved in **227 emergency department visits**; GHB was involved in 2,340 visits to the emergency department, according to the latest data from the Drug Abuse Warning Network (DAWN).

- In 2002 the Food and Drug Administration approved the only legal use of GHB: the **treatment of cataplexy**, a medical condition that causes a person's muscles to go suddenly limp.

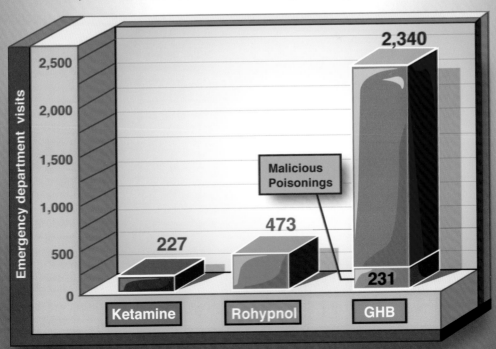

Emergency Room Visits Related to GHB, Ketamine, and Rohypnol

According to 2004 data from the Drug Abuse Warning Network, there were significantly fewer emergency department (ED) visits related to ketamine and Rohypnol compared to ED visits related to GHB. Out of 2,340 emergency department visits related to GHB, 231 were the result of malicious poisoning.

Rohypnol, GHB, and Ketamine: Prevalence of Use

Overall, student use of ketamine, Rohypnol, and GHB has decreased since 2000. According to the 2006 Monitoring the Future survey, 1.5 percent of students polled reported having used ketamine, Rohypnol, or GHB within the past twelve months.

Past year use of Rohypnol
(Percentage of students)

Grade	2000	2001	2002	2003	2004	2005	2006
Eighth grade	0.5	0.7	0.3	0.5	0.6	0.7	0.5
Tenth grade	0.8	1.0	0.7	0.6	0.7	0.5	0.5
Twelfth grade	0.8	0.9	1.6	1.3	1.6	1.2	1.1

Past year use of GHB
(Percentage of students)

Grade	2000	2001	2002	2003	2004	2005	2006
Eighth grade	1.2	1.1	0.8	0.9	0.7	0.5	0.8
Tenth grade	1.1	1.0	1.4	1.4	0.8	0.8	0.7
Twelfth grade	1.9	1.6	1.5	1.4	2.0	1.1	1.1

Past year use of Ketamine
(Percentage of students)

Grade	2000	2001	2002	2003	2004	2005	2006
Eighth grade	1.6	1.3	1.3	1.1	0.9	0.6	0.9
Tenth grade	2.1	2.1	2.2	1.9	1.3	1.0	1.0
Twelfth grade	2.5	2.5	2.6	2.1	1.9	1.6	1.4

Source: The Monitoring the Future study, the University of Michigan. www.monitoringthefuture.org.

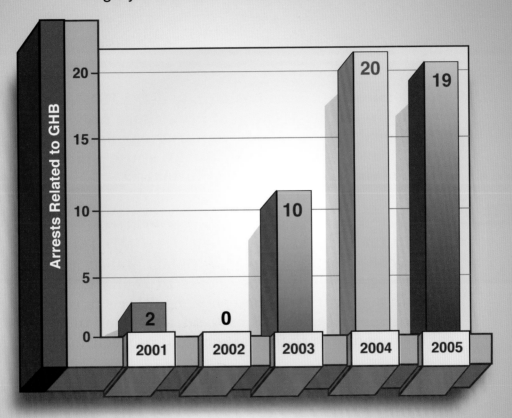

GHB-Related Arrests

Arrests related to GHB offenses are relatively rare, according to the Drug Enforcement Administration. No more than 20 arrests were made during any single year between 2001 and 2005.

Source: Drug Enforcement Administration. www.dea.gov.

- The **manufacturer of Rohypnol**, Hoffman-LaRoche, reformulated the drug to release a colored dye when mixed in liquid, making involuntary ingestion less likely.

- The **Drug Induced Rape & Punishment Act of 1996** and the Hillory J. Farias and Samantha Reid Date Rape Prohibition Act of 2000 increased the penalties for predators who employ date rape drugs.

How Can Club Drug Use Be Prevented?

66 More adolescents perceive harm in using MDMA than ever before, likely because of drug abuse prevention educational programs and antidrug campaigns that have focused on reducing MDMA abuse since the height of the drug's popularity in 2001. 99

—National Drug Intelligence Center, *National Drug Threat Assessment.*

66 Most of the risks associated with . . . [MDMA] are a direct consequence of prohibitionist public policy. These risks include poor access to realistic harm-reduction educational materials, health risks related to ingesting unregulated material, and delay in medical treatment due to fear of criminal prosecution. 99

—Jag Davies, "Ecstasy and Cheerleading: A Basic Risk Comparison."

I n 2001 President George Bush set an ambitious goal: to reduce youth drug use by 25 percent over a five-year period. Today, the president appears to have met or exceeded his goal; according to national surveillance data, the use of nearly every drug by the nation's youth is declining. Many credit the nation's drug control policy for these changes. As Attorney General Alberto R. Gonzales put it: "The Justice Department is committed to protecting teens from the destructive effects of drug use. Since 2001, we have seen the number of young people using drugs . . . steadily decline. These decreases are an encouraging sign that the Administration's ongoing efforts to combat drug abuse are helping America's children stay away from drugs."[21] Gonzales and others believe that these decreases are a direct result of the nation's three-pronged antidrug policy, which involves prevention, treatment, and law enforcement strategies that reduce the supply of club drugs and other illicit drugs available to young people.

Educational Programs

To many antidrug activists, preventing club drug abuse before it starts is the top priority of any drug control strategy. According to John P. Walters, director of the National Drug Control Policy, "We know that if people don't start using drugs during their teen years, they are very unlikely to go on to develop drug problems later in life."[22]

While educational programs that seek to prevent club drug use come in many forms, most use some form of media to proliferate antidrug messages. A television campaign targeting MDMA was launched by the Partnership for a Drug-Free America in 2002, for example. One of the organization's most compelling commercials focused on a young woman named Danielle who died after taking MDMA. In this spot, footage of Danielle as a healthy, vibrant youth was juxtaposed with solemn images of a coroner describing her autopsy. In a similar vein, anti-MDMA messages have been woven into the story lines of several popular television programs, including *The Sopranos, Law & Order,* and *ER.*

> While educational programs that seek to prevent club drug use come in many forms, most use some form of media to proliferate antidrug messages.

Similarly, the National Youth Anti-Drug Media Campaign, a program of the Office of National Drug Control Policy (ONDCP), implemented a campaign called "Above the Influence." Through judicious advertising in multiple venues that include television, Web sites, and school-based programs, the campaign seeks to make teens aware not only of the dangers of club drugs and other illicit substances, but also the influences that may lead to their abuse. To date, these and other programs continue to reach out to young people about the dangers of club drugs.

Harm Reduction

While educational campaigns that seek to empower young people to reject club drugs will undoubtedly continue, a far more controversial approach has garnered media attention in recent years: harm reduction, or strategies that mitigate the risks associated with illicit drug use. Those who promote harm reduction generally advocate the distribution of information and services that enable people to use recreational drugs as safely as possible. As DanceSafe, an organization that promotes harm reduction and works specifically within the rave and nightclub community, explains: "In its barest sense, harm reduction is a pragmatic approach to dealing with societal drug use. It begins with the observation that despite all our efforts as a society to stop the use of illicit drugs, people are using them anyway. . . . This necessitates a practical approach to reduce the harm that is taking place right now."[23]

To accomplish this, DanceSafe trains volunteers throughout the United States and Canada to staff harm reduction booths at raves and other dance venues. These volunteers distribute information on health and safety issues and provide pill-testing services that enable MDMA users to identify—and possibly avoid—fake or dangerously adulterated MDMA tablets. Because many medical emergencies at raves are the result of heat stroke, DanceSafe has implemented a number of guidelines that address the risk of overheating and dehydration. Rave organizers are exhorted, for example, to make bottled water available and to have adequate ventilation and chill-out rooms where patrons can go to cool down.

> " Those who promote harm reduction generally advocate the distribution of information and services that enable people to use recreational drugs as safely as possible. "

In general, these and other harm reduction measures continue to engender enormous controversy. Critics claim that there is little difference between harm reduction and promoting the use of these substances—and the harms associated with them. Walters is one vocal critic of harm reduction. As he describes those who ascribe to this philosophy, "Under the rubric of 'harm reduction,' they offer what is in effect an acquiescing to the disease of addiction, and suggest that we turn away from our responsibility to fight against the suffering."[24]

Anti-Rave Movement

Although all young people who attend raves do not use drugs, many believe that club drug use is inextricably linked with the rave setting. As one undercover narcotics detective put it, "We put on a drug-free rave in Florida. Three kids showed up."[25]

> **Many believe that club drug use is inextricably linked with the rave setting.**

In response, many communities in the late 1990s launched measures to reduce the number of raves—and curtail the use of club drugs associated with these events. Action took place on a number of fronts. To make it more difficult for rave organizers to operate, for example, law enforcement in many cities stepped up efforts to enforce existing laws such as juvenile curfews and liquor laws; other communities passed ordinances that rendered the production and promotion of raves—a potentially lucrative business—far less profitable. Cities such as Chicago, Denver, New York, and others, for example, started to require rave organizers to provide—and finance—emergency medical services and police security. Many of these measures proved successful. Faced with heightened scrutiny, increased costs, and the possibility of criminal penalties—many rave operations went out of business or moved to other locations.

One of the most effective antirave initiatives led to the demise of the largest rave operation in New Orleans in 2000. Dubbed "Operation Rave Review," this initiative utilized a two-pronged approach: First, the Drug Enforcement Administration (DEA) established a correlation between medical emergencies related to club drug and rave activity. Second, the DEA, in conjunction with New Orleans law enforcement, launched an investigation that primarily targeted rave promoters. Based on evidence that these organizers intentionally allowed the distribution of illegal drugs at their events, many were arrested, and the largest rave operation in the city came to a halt.

Overall, the prevalence of raves has subsided in recent years, partly as a result of Operation Rave Review and similar antirave initiatives. Many of these measures remain in place today to monitor and discourage raves and similar events that draw large numbers of young people.

> " Overall, the prevalence of raves has subsided in recent years, partly as a result of . . . antirave initiatives. "

Legislation

Several pieces of legislation address the manufacture, distribution, and possession of club drugs. One of the most significant is the U.S. Controlled Substances Act, passed by Congress in 1970. This legislation classifies all drugs into one of five groups, or schedules, according to their toxicity and potential for medical use. Schedule I drugs have the highest potential for abuse and no accepted medical use, whereas Schedule V drugs have a lower abuse potential and some acceptable medical use. Club drugs in the first category include MDMA, designated a Schedule I drug in 1985, and GHB, a Schedule I drug since 2000. Ketamine remains a Schedule III drug since it has legitimate medical value and a lower potential for abuse. Similarly, Rohypnol, a Schedule IV drug, has medical purposes outside of the United States. This scheduling system is related, in part, to prosecution. The penalty for the distribution of a Schedule I drug such as GHB, for example, is stiff; those found guilty can face many years in prison.

In recent years the federal government has taken other aggressive steps to curtail club drug use. The Ecstasy Anti-Proliferation Act of 2000, for example, greatly increased the penalties associated with the trafficking of MDMA and other club drugs. The Ecstasy Prevention Act, passed in 2001, strengthened the provisions of the Ecstasy Anti-Proliferation Act and allotted funding for antidrug programs. As Bob Graham, the Democratic senator from Florida who introduced the legislation, stated before Congress: "Through this campaign, our hope is that Ecstasy will soon go the way of crack, which saw a dramatic reduction in the quantities present on our streets after information of its unpredictable impurities and side effects were made known to a wide audience."[26]

The Rave Act

Perhaps the most controversial piece of legislation regarding club drugs is the Reducing Americans' Vulnerability to Ecstasy (RAVE) Act. First introduced in 2000 by Joseph Biden, a Democratic senator from Delaware and a vocal antidrug crusader, the legislation initially failed to pass. Renamed the Illicit Drug Anti-Proliferation Act and attached to the AMBER Alert Bill, legislation designed to improve child abduction investigations, the Rave Act became law in 2003.

The Rave Act specifically targets rave-style gatherings by penalizing property owners and business managers who fail to prevent illicit drug use on their property. According to Biden and other supporters, this legislation provides law enforcement and prosecutors necessary tools to combat illegal drug activity.

Conversely, the American Civil Liberties Union (ACLU) and other critics claim that the Rave Act violates constitutional rights: This act, they contend, creates an unfair legal standard. These critics claim that holding business owners and rave promoters legally liable for what some people choose to do is akin to "arresting the stadium owners and promoters of a Rolling Stones concert or a rap show because some concert-goers may be smoking or selling marijuana,"[27] as one ACLU spokesman put it.

Civil libertarians often cite another reason for opposing the Rave Act— that it unfairly targets and perhaps attempts to eradicate the entire culture of young people who gather to hear electronic music, just because this form of expression is sometimes associated with drug use.

> " The DEA and other organizations are working to curtail the availability of club drugs by disrupting their production and trafficking. "

Reducing the Supply of Club Drugs

In the United States the DEA and other organizations are working to curtail the availability of club drugs by disrupting their production and trafficking. The task is extremely difficult. MDMA trafficking, for example, is lucrative business, and the organizations that produce and deal

MDMA involve complex networks that are international in scope. Programs that target Rohypnol, ketamine, and GHB face similar problems.

In 2002 the DEA launched Operation X-Out, a year-long operation to eradicate organizations that produce and distribute MDMA and other club drugs. This initiative created multiple task forces, implemented procedures to enhance interdiction at airports and other ports of entry, and heightened cooperation with international drug agencies. At the same time, Operation X-Out teamed with a number of antidrug coalitions and civic and business leaders to bring public attention to the threat of club drugs.

Other initiatives have successfully removed MDMA and other club drugs from U.S. streets. Operation Candy Box, a three-year investigation launched by the DEA in 2001, resulted in the seizure of more than 700,000 MDMA tablets. More important, this operation dismantled a notorious MDMA ring headed by Ze Wai Wong, a Chinese national operating out of Canada. According to DEA administrator Karen Tandy, "The extradition of Ze Wai Wong to stand trial in the U.S. is a fitting conclusion to Wong's reign of preying on the U.S. with this dangerous drug that is primarily peddled to our youth. . . . Operation Candy Box decimated the U.S. MDMA market—dramatically reducing MDMA availability."[28] Similarly, the DEA announced in 2006 that its most recent initiative, Operation Triple Play, had crippled an MDMA trafficking organization that smuggled thousands of tablets from Canada to the streets of New York City.

Despite the success of these and other initiatives, the global production and trafficking of club drugs continues. In the years to come, antidrug authorities will surely use all the tools at their disposal to prevent what could become a glut in availability were club drug trafficking allowed to continue unabated.

How Can Club Drug Use Be Prevented?

> 66 The decrease in MDMA availability since 2001 likely is due to increasing interdiction efforts and the effective dismantling of large MDMA trafficking organizations. 99

—The National Drug Intelligence Center, *National Drug Threat Assessment*, 2005.

The National Drug Intelligence Center is a component of the U.S. Department of Justice. The *National Drug Threat Assessment* is its annual report on national trafficking and abuse trends.

> 66 The government's current anti-Ecstasy enforcement system, favored by law-and-order elected officials, clearly isn't working: Ecstasy's 'streetification' is happening despite a series of tough new laws aimed at cracking down harder on its use. 99

—Benjamin Wallace-Wells, "The Agony of Ecstasy," *Washington Monthly*, May 2003.

Wallace-Wells is an editor for the *Washington Monthly*.

Primary Source Quotes

❝ The reason for the decline [in ecstasy] is simple: education. The medium: television. More and more kids now know that ecstasy is dangerous thanks to a message that is being hammered home on the tube. ❞

—*WSJ.com*, "Teen Ecstasy," February 27, 2004.

WSJ.com is an online version of the *Wall Street Journal*, one of the world's leading sources of news and business information.

❝ Club drugs have become an integral part of the rave scene. . . . The open distribution of MDMA and other club drugs has become commonplace at many of these venues. ❞

—Asa Hutchinson, testimony before the House Government Reform Subcommittee on Criminal Justice, Drug Policy, and Human Resources, September 19, 2002.

Hutchinson is the former administrator of the Drug Enforcement Administration (DEA). During his tenure the DEA identified MDMA and other club drugs as an emerging drug threat and focused federal resources on curtailing their use.

❝ The use of . . . "club drugs" within the electronic music community is neither widespread nor disproportionate to the consumption of these drugs by other communities in other settings. ❞

—Drug Policy Alliance, "Legal Defense of Electronic Music," 2007. www.drugpolicy.org.

The Drug Policy Alliance is an organization working to reform the current war on drugs.

66Users of each of the club drugs tend to be very different in terms of sociodemographic characteristics, patterns of multiple drug use, and reasons for use. . . . Prevention and treatment efforts should be tailored to these specific differences.**99**

—Jane Carlisle Maxwell, "Patterns of Club Drug Use in the U.S.," Gulf Coast Addiction Technology Transfer Center, 2004.

Maxwell is a research professor at the University of Texas at Austin.

66[Federal officials should] focus attention on the promoters and operators of rave events that facilitate the trafficking and abuse of MDMA and other club drugs.**99**

—Drug Enforcement Administration, "National Synthetic Drugs Action Plan," 2004. www.dea.gov.

The Drug Enforcement Administration, a branch of the Justice Department, is the nation's chief antidrug enforcement agency.

66Some people use drugs at some raves, just like some people use drugs at rock concerts, sporting events, and state fairs. Singling out one type of event and one type of music is unfair and un-American.**99**

—American Civil Liberties Union, "DEA Must Not Be Allowed to Chill Speech or Shut Down Electronic Music Events," September 11, 2003. www.aclu.org.

The ACLU is an organization committed to defending the principles of free speech and other civil liberties.

"Rave party problems are but the latest variation in an ongoing history of problems associated with youth entertainment, experimentation, rebellion, and self discovery."

—Michael S. Scott, "Rave Parties," *Problem-Oriented Guides for Police*, August 2004.

Scott is an independent police consultant and the author *of Problem-Oriented Guides for Police*, written in association with the U.S. Department of Justice. The guide is distributed to law enforcement officers to inform them about specific crimes and disorder problems associated with raves in their communities.

"Rather than eliminating drug use or even entirely eliminating raves, the . . . [Rave Act will] drive raves underground and discourage basic health precautions. It would have the perverse effect of making drug use more dangerous."

—Graham Boyd, testimony before the House Judiciary Subcommittee on Crime, Terrorism, and Homeland Security, October 10, 2002.

Boyd is the director of the American Civil Liberties Union Drug Policy Litigation Project.

"[The Rave Act] will take steps to educate youth, parents and other interested adults about the dangers of Ecstasy and other club drugs associated with raves."

—Joseph R. Biden Jr., statement before the U.S. Senate, January 28, 2003.

Biden is the Democratic senator who introduced the Rave Act in 2002.

66 An effective Ecstasy campaign should be designed to save lives and reduce health problems, rather than merely preaching total abstinence, which might not be the choice of all individuals. **99**

—Marsha Rosenbaum, "Ecstasy: America's New Reefer Madness," *Journal of Psychoactive Drugs*, April–June 2002.

Rosenbaum is the director of the San Francisco office of the Drug Policy Alliance.

How Can Club Drug Use Be Prevented?

- When club drug **use spiked** in the 1990s, the ONDCP, NIDA, and other organizations implemented extensive media campaigns to educate young people about the dangers of these drugs.

- One of the principal goals of harm reduction—efforts to **minimize the dangers** of club drugs—is to remind young people to stay cool and well hydrated if they choose to ingest MDMA.

- At raves and similar venues, **harm reduction organizations** provide on-site pill testing to determine the purity of MDMA tablets.

- Many law enforcement agencies and antidrug officials contend that harm reduction organizations **encourage illicit drug use**.

- The **prevalence of raves has subsided** since the turn of the twenty-first century.

- Law enforcement agencies in many cities have **reduced rave activity** by strictly enforcing fire codes and other public safety ordinances.

- The Ecstasy Anti-Proliferation Act of 2000 increased the penalties for trafficking MDMA: The sentence for trafficking **800 MDMA pills** increased from 15 months to 5 years.

Is MDMA Use Associated with Other Illicit Drug Use?

According to the National Survey on Drug Use and Health, individuals who had used MDMA during the past year were far more likely to have also used alcohol or other drugs. Only 9.1 percent of MDMA users reported not using other illicit drugs during the past year, compared with 86.2 percent of individuals who did not use MDMA.

	Percentage of persons who reported past year MDMA use	Percentage of persons who reported no past year MDMA use
No Illicit Drug Use During Past Year (Other than MDMA)	9.1%	86.2%
Illicit Drug Use During Past Year		
Alcohol	97.5%	65.2%
Any illicit drug	90.9%	13.8%
Marijuana	85.0%	9.9%
Prescription pain relievers*	45.6%	4.3%
Cocaine	43.8%	2.0%
Prescription tranquilizers*	28.7%	1.8%
Prescription stimulants*	22.1%	1.0%
LSD	16.8%	0.1%
Inhalants	14.7%	0.7%
PCP	5.2%	0.0%
Prescription sedatives*	3.6%	0.3%
Heroin	3.2%	0.1%

*nonmedical use

Source: SAMHSA/2003 National Survey on Drug Use and Health.

Average Age of First-Time Illicit Drug Users

This graph shows the average age of first-time users of MDMA and other recreational drugs. Because users of illicit substances are often young, many prevention programs target high school students and other youth groups.

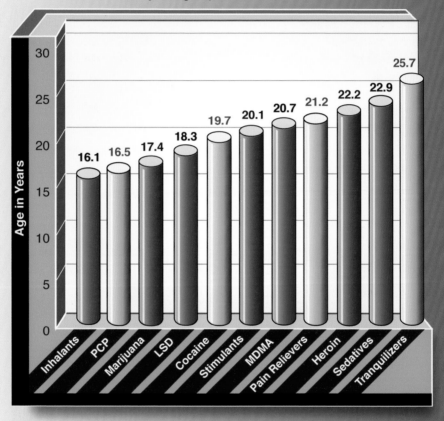

Source: SAMHSA/2005 National Survey on Drug Use and Health.

- The **Illicit Drug Anti-Proliferation Act of 2003** holds business owners and rave promoters responsible—and liable for thousands of dollars in fines—for the drug use of their patrons.

- The **American Civil Liberties Union (ACLU)** and similar organizations contend that antirave legislation threatens young people's constitutional right to musical expression and the right to gather and dance.

- The DEA has launched several initiatives, including **Operation Candy Box** and **Operation Triple Play**, which have successfully eradicated a number of club drug trafficking organizations.

Trends in Availability of MDMA

According to data from the most recent Monitoring the Future study, it is becoming increasingly difficult for young people to acquire MDMA on the street. The number of eighth-, tenth-, and twelfth-graders who report that MDMA is "fairly easy" or "very easy" to get has declined significantly since 2001.

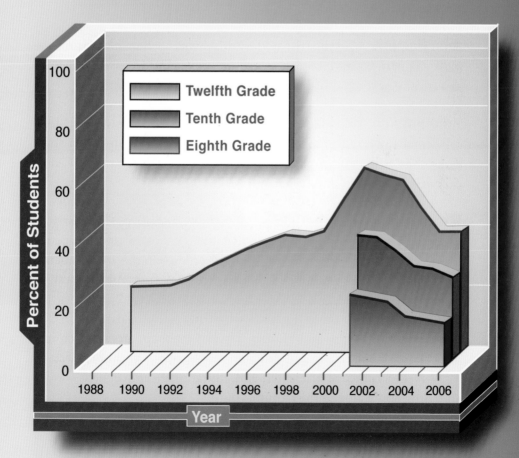

Source: The Monitoring the Future study, the University of Michigan. www.monitoringthefuture.org.

Key People and Advocacy Groups

Rick Doblin: Doblin is a vocal advocate of MDMA-assisted psychotherapy. Through the organization that he founded, the Multidisciplinary Association for Psychedelic Studies (MAPS), Doblin lobbies for FDA-approved human tests studies on the risks and benefits of MDMA and assists current research efforts.

John Greer: Perhaps the best-known doctor to administer MDMA in a clinical, therapeutic setting, Greer prescribed it to at least 80 patients suffering from anxiety and depression before the drug became a controlled substance in 1985.

John Halpern: A psychiatrist at Harvard Medical School's McLean Hospital, Halpern is conducting research to assess MDMA-assisted therapy as a treatment for end-of-life anxiety in terminal cancer patients.

Julie Holland: Holland is a psychiatrist at New York University Medical Center and is one of the foremost experts on MDMA and other street drugs. She is the editor of *Ecstasy: The Complete Guide,* a widely cited overview of the risks and benefits of MDMA.

Michael Mithoefer: Mithoefer is a South Carolina psychiatrist who is conducting the first FDA-approved human study on the therapeutic use of MDMA for post-traumatic stress disorder. Subjects in Mithoefer's study include crime victims and soldiers returning from the Iraq war.

National Institute on Drug Abuse (NIDA): NIDA is part of the U.S. Department of Health and Human Services that supports research into drug abuse and addiction and disseminates the results of this research. In 1999 NIDA launched a research and educational campaign to combat club drug abuse among the nation's youth.

Trinka Porrata: Porrata is a former Los Angeles police detective and nationally recognized expert on GHB. Through her Web site Project GHB,

Porrata disseminates information about GHB and other club drugs. She worked with the DEA to enact legislation that made GHB a Schedule I drug.

George Ricaurte: A neurologist at the Johns Hopkins School of Medicine, Ricaurte has conducted extensive research on the neurotoxicity of MDMA.

Alexander "Sasha" Shulgin: Shulgin is a chemist and long-time psychedelic advocate. The first to synthesize MDMA for recreational use, Shulgin popularized the drug in the 1970s, especially as a treatment for depression and other psychological ailments.

Karen Tandy: As administrator of the federal Drug Enforcement Administration, Tandy is charged with implementing the current administration's war on drugs. In recent years, Tandy has overseen several DEA operations that targeted—and dismantled—a number of illegal club drug trafficking rings.

Nora Volkow: Volkow is one of the country's foremost addiction researchers and the director of the National Institute on Drug Abuse. An expert on the brain's dopamine system, Volkow has conducted extensive brain imaging studies on the effects of MDMA and other drugs.

John P. Walters: Walters is the director of the White House Office of National Drug Control Policy. As the nation's "drug czar," Walters oversees all federal drug programs including the National Youth Anti-Drug Media Campaign, which partners with other organizations to reduce drug use and addiction.

Chronology

1970s
Alexander Shulgin begins experiments with MDMA and introduces the drug to a small group of psychotherapists. Use of ketamine as a human anesthetic declines.

1980s
MDMA's popularity as a recreational drug burgeons. The drug is openly distributed in bars and nightclubs in Dallas, Austin, and Ft. Worth, Texas. GHB is sold over the counter in health food stores.

1960
French scientist Henri-Marie Laborit first synthesizes GHB as an anesthetic agent.

Late 1970s
An underground group of psychotherapists uses MDMA as a therapeutic adjunct.

1983
First rave-style party is held on the island of Ibiza in Spain.

1990
The Federal Drug Administration (FDA) bans over-the-counter sales of GHB.

1912
MDMA first synthesized by German pharmaceutical company E. Merck.

1900　　**1960**　　**1970**　　**1980**　　**1990**

1961
Ketamine is developed as a human and animal anesthetic.

1985
MDMA is placed under a one-year Schedule I emergency ban, classifying MDMA as a drug with "no legitimate medical use and high potential for abuse."

1988
MDMA is removed from Schedule I in January and returned in March. As the British rave scene grows in popularity, the "summer of love," marked by heavy MDMA consumption, takes place in Great Britain.

Late 1960s
MDA, an analog of MDMA, is popularized as a recreational drug.

Early 1990s
The rave scene takes root in major U.S. metropolitan areas; the movement spreads to almost every U.S. state. Recreational use of ketamine and Rohypnol increase.

1978
Alexander Shulgin and David Nichols publish first paper documenting the effects of MDMA on humans.

1986
The Multidisciplinary Association for Psychedelic Studies (MAPS) begins research on MDMA. Nancy Reagan spearheads the "Just Say No" antidrug campaign.

1995

In England 18-year-old Leah Betts dies after ingesting too much water to counteract the effects of MDMA. Her parents allow her deathbed pictures to be used in anti-Ecstasy campaigns, sparking public outrage against MDMA.

1999

Ketamine is added to Schedule III, for drugs with the potential for abuse. The National Institute on Drug Abuse launches a multimillion-dollar multimedia campaign to alert young people to the dangers of club drugs.

2003

The Illicit Drug Anti-Proliferation Act, with provisions of the Rave Act, becomes law. George Ricaurte retracts his 2002 study on the grounds that methamphetamine rather than MDMA was administered.

1996

The Drug-Induced Rape Prevention Act passes.

Early 2000s

Researchers at the National Institute of Mental Health begin studying ketamine as a treatment for depression.

1995   1998   2001   2004   2007

1997

Rohypnol manufacturer Hoffman-LaRoche reformulates the drug to turn blue when mixed with beverages, making it easier to detect.

2000

The Club Drug Act becomes law. U.S. Customs reports seizing 9.3 million doses of MDMA. The Hillory J. Farias and Samantha Reid Date-Rape Prohibition Act of 1999 is signed.

2004

Michael Mithoefer launches the first of several FDA-approved human studies to assess MDMA-assisted therapy as a treatment for anxiety and post-traumatic stress disorder.

1998

George Ricaurte of Johns Hopkins University sparks controversy when he publishes a study suggesting that MDMA damages the brain's serotonin system.

2002

The Rave Act fails to pass Congress. George Ricaurte publishes animal research suggesting that MDMA may cause Parkinson's disease. The FDA approves the use of GHB as a treatment for cataplexy.

Early 2007

A study in Israel on MDMA-assisted therapy for war- and terrorism-related post-traumatic stress disorder begins to enroll subjects. Authorities in Switzerland approve MDMA for clinical trials.

Related Organizations

DanceSafe

536 45th St.

Oakland, CA 94609

e-mail: dsusa@dancesafe.org

Web site: www.dancesafe.org

DanceSafe is a harm reduction organization created specifically to promote public health and safety within the rave and nightclub circuit. With chapters throughout the United Sates and Canada, DanceSafe volunteers provide drug information and pill-testing services at raves and other dance events.

Drug Enforcement Administration (DEA)

2401 Jefferson Davis Hwy., Suite 300

Alexandria, VA 22301

phone: (800) 882-9539

Web site: www.dea.gov

The Drug Enforcement Administration works to enforce the nation's drug laws. It coordinates the activities of federal, state, and local agencies and works with governments outside of the United States to curtail the smuggling and distribution of illicit drugs in the nation.

Drug Free America Foundation

2600 9th St. N., Suite 200

St. Petersburg, FL 33704

phone: (727) 828-0211

fax: (727) 828-0212

Web site: www.dfaf.org

Drug Free America Foundation is a drug prevention organization that supports global strategies, policies, and legislation to reduce drug abuse and addiction. The foundation promotes abstinence-only drug education.

Drug Policy Alliance

925 15th St. NW, 2nd Floor

Washington, DC 20005

phone: (202) 216-0035

fax: (202) 216-0803

e-mail: dc@drugpolicy.org

Web site: www.drugpolicy.org

The Drug Policy Alliance promotes alternatives to the nation's current drug policies and enforcement measures. The alliance works to reduce the harms associated with drug use through syringe exchange, science-based drug education, and other programs.

Drug Reform Coordination Network

1623 Connecticut Ave. NW, 3rd Floor

Washington, DC 20009

phone: (202) 293-8340

fax: (202) 293-8344

e-mail: drcnet@drcnet.org

Web site: http://stopthedrugwar.org

The Drug Reform Coordination Network is an international organization that calls for an end to drug prohibition. The network seeks to replace current drug laws with a program through which illicit drugs can be regulated and controlled.

Erowid

PO Box 1116

Grass Valley, CA 95945

e-mail: sage@erowid.org

Web site: www.erowid.org

Erowid is an online library that provides information on the chemical composition, distribution, and physical effects of psychoactive drugs and related issues.

Multidisciplinary Association for Psychedelic Studies (MAPS)

10,424 Love Creek Rd.

Ben Lomond, CA 95005

phone: (831) 336-4325

fax: (831) 336-3665

e-mail: askmaps@maps.org

Web site: www.maps.org

MAPS is a research and educational organization that advocates the "beneficial, socially sanctioned uses of psychedelic drugs." To this end, MAPS supports research on human subjects to determine the efficacy and safety of MDMA when used in a medical treatment setting.

National Center on Addiction and Substance Abuse at Columbia University (CASA)

633 3rd Ave., 19th Floor

New York, NY 10017-6706

phone: (212) 841-5200

Web site: www.casacolumbia.org

CASA is a nonprofit organization that distributes information about the dangers of drug abuse and addiction. It formulates substance abuse prevention and treatment strategies to help curb the problem of illicit drug abuse.

National Institute on Drug Abuse (NIDA)

6001 Executive Blvd., Room 5213

Bethesda, MD 20892

phone: (301) 443-1124

e-mail: information@nida.nih.gov

Web site: www.nida.nih.gov

NIDA is part of the National Institutes of Health, a branch of the Department of Health and Human Services. It both supports and conducts extensive scientific research on drug abuse and addiction. By disseminating its research findings, NIDA hopes to prevent drug abuse, improve treatment options, and influence public policy.

Office of National Drug Control Policy (ONDCP)

PO Box 6000

Rockville, MD 20849-6000

phone: (800) 666-3332

fax: (301) 519-5212

Web site: www.whitehousedrugpolicy.gov

The White House Office of National Drug Control Policy was established to formulate and implement the nation's drug control program. The goals of the program are to reduce illicit drug use and drug-related trafficking, crime, and violence.

Partnership for a Drug-Free America

405 Lexington Ave., Suite 1601

New York, NY 10174

phone: (212) 922-1560

fax: (212) 922-1570

Web site: www.drugfreeamerica.org

The Partnership for a Drug-Free America is a nonprofit organization that works to educate the public, particularly young people, about the dangers of drug abuse. Through extensive media campaigns, the partnership hopes to spread its antidrug message and prevent drug abuse among the nation's youths.

Project GHB, Inc.

556 S. Fair Oaks, No. 101–178

Pasadena, CA 91105

e-mail: trinka@projectghb.org

Web site: www.projectghb.org

Project GHB seeks to educate young people on the dangers of GHB and other club drugs. Largely through its Web site, Project GHB disseminates information on club drugs and publishes personal stories of GHB addiction and overdose.

For Further Research

Books

Julie Holland, ed., *Ecstasy: The Complete Guide: A Comprehensive Look at the Risks and Benefits of MDMA.* Rochester, VT: Park Street, 2001.

Karl Jansen, *Ketamine: Dreams and Realities.* Sarasota, FL: Multidisciplinary Association for Psychedelic Studies, 2004.

Philip Jenkins, *Synthetic Panics: The Symbolic Politics of Designer Drugs.* New York: New York University Press, 1999.

Cynthia R. Knowles, *Up All Night: A Closer Look at Club Drugs and Rave Culture.* Geneseo, NY: Red House, 2001.

Cynthia Kuhn, Scott Swartzwelder, and Wilkie Wilson, *Buzzed: The Straight Facts About the Most Used and Abused Drugs from Alcohol to Ecstasy.* New York: W.W. Norton, 1998.

Tara McCall, *This Is Not a Rave: In the Shadow of a Subculture.* New York: Thunder's Mouth, 2001.

James N. Parker and Philip M. Parker, eds., *The Official Patient's Sourcebook on GHB Dependence: A Revised and Updated Directory for the Internet Age.* San Diego: Icon Health, 2002.

Scott W. Perkins, *Drug Identification: Designer and Club Drugs Quick Reference Guide.* Carrolton, TX: Alliance, 2000.

Simon Reynolds, *Generation Ecstasy: Into the World of Techno and Rave Culture.* New York: Routledge, 1999.

Salvatore J. Salamone, ed., *Benzodiazepines and GHB: Detection and Pharmacology.* Totowa, NJ: Humana, 2001.

Lynn Marie Smith, *Rolling Away: My Agony with Ecstasy.* New York: Atria, 2005.

Gareth Thomas, *The Little Book of Ecstasy.* London: Sanctuary, 2003.

Sarah Thornton, *Club Cultures: Music, Media, and Subculture Capital.* Cambridge: Polity, 1995.

Periodicals

Melissa Abramovitz, "The Knockout Punch of Date Rape Drugs," *Current Health*, March 1, 2001.

Karen Breslau, Ashley Fantz, and Kevin Peraino, "The 'Sextasy' Craze," *Newsweek*, June 3, 2002.

John Cloud, "The Lure of Ecstasy," *Time*, June 5, 2000.

Eve Conant, "Ecstasy: A Possible New Role for a Banned Drug," *Newsweek*, May 2, 2005.

H.V. Curran and L. Monaghan, "In and Out of the K-Hole: A Comparison of the Acute and Residual Effects of Ketamine in Frequent and Infrequent Ketamine Users," *Addiction*, vol. 96, 2001.

Jonathan Darman, "Out of the Club, onto the Couch," *Newsweek*, December 5, 2003.

John DePresca, "Date Rape Drugs," *Law and Order*, October 1, 2003.

P. Dillon, J. Copeland, and K. Jansen, "Patterns of Use and Harms Associated with Non-Medical Ketamine Use," *Drug and Alcohol Dependence*, 2003.

Paul M. Gahlinger, "Club Drugs—Myths and Risks," *American Family Physician*, June 1, 2004.

Kurt Kleiner, "Why Not Just Say Yes?" *New Scientist*, August 9, 2003.

Jane Carlisle Maxwell, "Party Drugs: Properties, Prevalence, Patterns, and Problems," *Substance Use and Misuse*, vol. 40, 2005.

T. McKusick, "Catch a Rave," *Utne Reader*, September/October 1996.

Donald G. McNeil Jr., "Research on Ecstasy Is Clouded by Errors," *New York Times*, December 2, 2003.

Tamar Nordenberg, "The Death of the Party," *FDA Consumer Magazine*, vol. 34, March/April 2000.

Susan Oh and Ruth Atherley, "Rave Fever: Kids Love Those All Night Parties," *Maclean's*, April 24, 2000.

Science World, "The Agony of Ecstasy," February 26, 2001.

Wyre Sententia, "Your Mind Is a Target," *Humanist*, January/February 2003.

Carla Spartos, "The Ecstasy Factor," *Village Voice*, March 10, 2004.

Kerri Wachter, "What You Need to Know About Club Drugs: Rave On," *Family Practice News*, November 15, 2003.

Shirley Wang, "Radical Relief," *Philadelphia Enquirer*, August 22, 2005.

Internet Sources

Drug Enforcement Administration, "MDMA (Ecstasy)," August 2006. www.dea.gov/concern/mdma.html.

Drug Policy Alliance, "Club Drugs," 2007. www.drugpolicy.org/drugby drug/clubdrugs.

National Drug Intelligence Center, *National Drug Threat Assessment 2007.* www.usdoj.gov/ndic/pubs21/21137/index.htm.

National Institute on Drug Abuse, "NIDA InfoFacts: Club Drugs," May 2006. www.drugabuse.gov/infofacts/Clubdrugs.html.

National Institute on Drug Abuse, *Research Report: MDMA (Ecstasy) Abuse,"* March 2006. www.drugabuse.gov/ResearchReports/MDMA.

Office of National Drug Control Policy, "Club Drugs," February 27, 2007. www.whitehousedrugpolicy.gov/drugfact/club/index.html.

Source Notes

Overview

1. Heather Morgan, "Rave Inside 90s Counter-Culture." www.bouldernews. com.
2. Tara McCall, *This Is Not a Rave: In the Shadow of a Subculture.* New York: Thunder's Mouth, 2001, p. 4.
3. Cynthia R. Knowles, *Up All Night: A Closer Look at Club Drugs and Rave Culture.* New York: Red House, 2001, p. viii.
4. Quoted in Jacob Sullum, "Sex, Drugs and Techno Music: Why the Rap Against Ecstasy Has a Familiar Ring to It," *Reason*, January 2002.
5. Julie Holland, ed., *Ecstasy: The Complete Guide.* Rochester, VT: Park Street, 2001, p. 3.
6. Philip Jenkins, *Synthetic Panics: The Symbolic Politics of Designer Drugs.* New York: New York University Press, 1999, p. 88.
7. Jenkins, *Synthetic Panics*, p. 3.
8. Asa Hutchinson, statement to National Foundation for Women's Legislators Press Conference, May 23, 2002.

How Harmful Is MDMA?

9. Nicole Hansen, "Real Drugs, False Friends," January 13, 2005. wwwdrugfree.org.
10. Drugstory.org, "Undercover at Teen Raves: An Interview with Joe Ryan," 2007. www.drugstory.org.
11. Lynn Marie Smith, "Agony from Ecstasy," January 14, 2005. www.drugfree. org.
12. Quoted in Linda Marsa, "The Highs and Lows of Ecstasy," *Los Angeles Times*, July 16, 2001.

How Do Club Drugs Affect Society?

13. Quoted in PBS, "In the Mix: Ecstasy," April 7–14, 2001. www.pbs.org.
14. Quoted in Laura D'Angelo, "E Is for Empty: Daniel's Story," *Scholastic, Inc.*, 2003.
15. Smith, "Agony from Ecstasy."
16. TheDEA.org, "Ecstasy: An Abridged FAQ for Medical Personnel and Assorted Science Geeks," May 2003. http://thedea.org.
17. Gareth Thomas, *This Is Ecstasy.* London: Sanctuary, 2002.

How Can Date Rape Drugs Be Controlled?

18. Tracy Duffy and Tina Whelan, "The Truth About 'Date Rape' Drugs." www. coalitionagainstviolence.ca.
19. Nora Fitzgerald and K. Jack Riley, "Drug-Facilitated Rape: Looking for the Missing Pieces," *National Institute of Justice Journal*, April 2000.
20. John DePresca, "Date Rape Drugs," *Law & Order*, October 2003.

How Can Club Drug Use Be Prevented?

21. Office of National Drug Control Policy, "Teen Drug Use Declines 23 Percent in Five Years, Marijuana, Meth Use Drop Sharply," December 21, 2006. www. whitehousedrugpolicy.gov.
22. National Institute on Drug Abuse, "NIDA-Sponsored Survey Shows Decrease in Illicit Drug Use Among Nation's Teens, but Prescription Drug

Abuse Remains High," December 21, 2006. www.nida.nih.gov.

23. DanceSafe, "Philosophy and Vision." http://dancesafe.org.

24. John P. Walters, "A Compassionate but Effective Drug Control Policy," March 1, 2005. www.whitehousedrugpolicy.gov.

25. Roy Rutland, "Ecstasy and Club Drugs," comments at roundtable discussion sponsored by the National Youth Anti-Drug Media Campaign.

26. Bob Graham, statement before U.S. Senate Committee on the Judiciary, July 19, 2001. www.cognitiveliberty.org.

27. American Civil Liberties Union, "Censorship Is Latest Drug War Tactic as Government Seeks to Put 'Rave' Dance Music Promoters in Prison," March 7, 2001. www.aclu.org.

28. Drug Enforcement Administration, "DEA Finds Significant Nationwide Impact as a Result of International Ecstasy Investigation," January 18, 2005. www.usdoj.gov/dea.

List of Illustrations

How Harmful Is MDMA?

Drug-Related Emergency Room Visits   37
Cheerleading and Recreational MDMA Use: A Risk Analysis   38
Average Purity of Drug Samples   39
Addiction Potential of Illicit Drugs   40

How Do Club Drugs Affect Society?

How Many Students Have Used MDMA?   54
Illicit Drug Use   55
How Great a Threat Is MDMA to Authorities?   56
MDMA-Related Arrests   57
GHB and MDMA Laboratory Seizures   58

How Can Date Rape Drugs Be Controlled?

Emergency Room Visits Related to GHB, Ketamine, and Rohypnol   73
Rohypnol, GHB, and Ketamine: Prevalence of Use   74
GHB-Related Arrests   75

How Can Club Drug Use Be Prevented?

Is MDMA Use Associated with Other Illicit Drug Use?   89
Average Age of First-Time Illicit Drug Users   90
Trends in Availability of MDMA   91

Index

addiction, potential for
  to illicit drugs, 40 (chart)
  MDMA, 27
American Civil Liberties Union
  (ACLU), 81, 85, 90
amnesia, from date rape drugs,
  60, 62, 72
Appleton, Josie, 69

Bartlett, Thomas, 33
benzodiazepines, 18
Biden, Joseph R., Jr., 86
black market, 45
Blysma, Tony, 10
Boyd, Benjamin, 86
Buoso, Jose Carlos, 51
Bush, George W., 76

Chambers, Britney, 26
Clinton, Bill, 63
club drugs
  assessing threat of, 47–48
  decline in use of, 53
  definition of, 10–11
  prevalence in use of, 41–42
  reducing supply of, 81–82
  risky behaviors associated
    with, 44–45
  sexual risk taking and,
    43–44

societal effects of, 19–20, 50
typical users of, 42–43, 85
see also GHB; ketamine;
  MDMA; Rohypnol
cocaine, average purity of, 39
  (chart)
Concar, David, 34
Controlled Substances Act,
  U.S. (1970), 80
crime
  date rape drugs and, 72
  Ecstasy and, 50
  implications of club drugs
    in, 9

DanceSafe, 78
date rape drugs, 20–21, 44
Davies, Jag, 76
DePresca, John, 70
depression, association with
  MDMA use, 8, 17, 25, 36,
  44
Doblin, Rick, 23, 28, 31
dopamine, 24
Drink Detective, 68
Drug Abuse Warning Network
  (DAWN), 61
Drug Enforcement
  Administration (DEA), 15,
  65, 67, 82, 85

on prevalence of MDMA
    use, 41
Drug Induced Rape and
    Punishment Act (1996), 63,
    75
Drug Policy Alliance, 32, 70,
    84
drugs, illicit
    addiction potential of, 40
        (chart)
    average first time use of, 90
        (chart)
    average purity of, 39 (chart)
    emergency room visits
        related to, 37 (chart)
    MDMA use and use of other,
        89 (chart)
    prevalence in use of, among
        youth, 55 (chart)
    significance of threat from,
        56 (chart)
DrugStory.org, 50
du-Cille, Jessica, 69
Duffy, Tracy, 59, 69

Ecstasy. *See* MDMA
Ecstasy Anti-Proliferation Act
    (2000), 8, 80
emergency room visits
    from club drugs, 73 (chart)
    drug-related, 37 (chart),
        61–62
    relating to MDMA vs.
        cheerleading injuries, 38
        (chart)

Farias, Hillory J., 63
Fitzgerald, Nora, 61
flunitrazepam. See Rohypnol
Food and Drug Administration,
    U.S. (FDA), 15

Gerstein, Dean R., 50
GHB (gamma-hydroxybutyrate),
    10–11, 52
    arrests related to, 56, 75
        (chart)
    as date rape drug, 60, 67, 70
    effects of, 17
    laboratory seizures of, 58
        (chart)
    metabolism of, 72
    prevalence of use among
        students, 74 (chart)
    trafficking of, 47
Gilbride, John P., 51
Gonzalez, Alberto R., 76
Graham, Bob, 80
Grinspoon, Lester, 29

Halpern, John, 30
Hansen, Nicole, 34
harm reduction programs,
    78–79, 88
health effects
    of GHB, 17
    of ketamine, 19
    of MDMA, 8, 16–17,
        24–26, 27–29
    of Rohypnol, 19

Hendrickson, James C., 50

Hillory J. Farias and Samantha Reid Date Rape Prevention Act, 8, 63–64

Hutchinson, Asa, 20, 84

Illicit Drug Anti-Proliferation Act (2003), 81, 90

Jenkins, Philip, 14–15

ketamine, 9, 11, 19
  as date rape drug, 60
  emergency room visits related to, 73 (chart)
  prevalence of use among students, 74 (chart)
  sources of, 53
  trafficking of, 47
Kish, Stephen, 35
Knowles, Cynthia R., 13–14
law enforcement
  challenges to, from date rape drugs, 62–63
  drugs identified as major threat by, 48, 56 (chart)
  impact of black market on, 45
LSD, 11

Maxwell, Jane Carlisle, 10, 85
MDMA (methylene-dioxymethamphetamine), 8, 10, 13

addition potential of, 27
alteration of, 26
arrests related to, 56, 57 (chart)
association with other illicit drug use, 89 (chart)
availability of, 22, 52
  trends in, 91 (chart)
average purity of, 39 (chart)
biological effects of, 23–24
clinical trials of, 15, 29–30
crime associated with, 53
crimes associated with, 48
effects of, 15–16, 24–26
emergency room visits related to, 73 (chart)
first synthesis of, 14
laboratory seizures of, 58 (chart)
link between brain damage and, 27–29
prevalence in use of, among students, 54 (chart)
research on, 9
significance of threat from, 56 (chart)
trafficking of, 45–47
TV campaign targeting, 77
use with other drugs, 26–27
methamphetamine, 11
  average purity of, 39 (chart), 46
Mithoefer, Michael, 30, 33

Monitoring the Future (MTF) study, 19, 42, 54, 62, 74

Multidisciplinary Association for Psychedelic Studies (MAPS), 28

Narconon, 41, 49
National Bureau of Crime Statistics, 62
National Drug Intelligence Center, 52, 59, 76, 83
National Institute on Drug Abuse (NIDA), 19, 23, 36, 61
National Survey on Drug Use and Health (NSDUH), 42
National Youth Anti-Drug Media Campaign, 77
Negrusz, Adam, 71
neurotransmitters, effects of MDMA on, 8, 23–24
Novoa, Robert A., 51

Office of Diversion Control, 52
Office of National Drug Control Policy (ONDCP), 22 [Ed: "Office of" missing here], 43, 77, 88
spending by, 45
Operation Candy Box, 82
Operation Rave Review, 79–80
Operation Triple Play, 82

Operation X-Out, 82

Partnership for a Drug-Free America, 21, 77
Pinsky, David Drew, 33
post-traumatic stress disorder, MDMA as treatment for, 38
prevention/education programs, 21–22, 77–78, 88
federal, 76–77
for date rape drugs, 63–64
Project GHB, 52

Rankman, Angie, 68
rave culture, 12–14
decline in, 88
movement against, 79–80
Reducing Americans' Vulnerability to Ecstasy (RAVE) Act (proposed), 81
Ricaurte, George, 28
Rilery, K. Jack, 61
Rohypnol (flunitrazepam), 9, 11, 18–19, 54
as date rape drug, 60, 67, 70
emergency room visits related to, 73 (chart)
improved detection for, 65–66
metabolism of, 72
prevalence of use among students, 74 (chart)

trafficking of, 47
Rose, Pete, Jr., 43
Rosenbaum, Marsh, 49, 87

Scott, Michael S., 41, 86
serotonin, 24, 27, 36
sexual assaults, 59
  drug-facilitated, prevalence
    of, 61–62
Shulgin, Alexander "Sasha," 14
Smith, Lynn Marie, 34
Sullum, Jacob, 32, 68
Swiss Physicians Against Drugs,
  32

TheDEA.org, 59
Thomas, Gareth, 46, 52

Valium, 18
Volkow, Nora, 31, 50

Wallace-Wells, Benjamin, 83
Walters, John P., 77, 78
"Watch Your Drink–Watch
  Your Friend" campaign,
  64–65, 67
Whelan, Tina, 59, 69
Wong, Ze Wai, 82
WSJ.com, 84

About the Author

Jill Karson is a graduate of the University of California at Irvine. A freelance editor and writer, Karson lives in Carlsbad, California, with her husband, Jack, and three children, Damon, Drew, and Olivia.